Illustrated Guide to Classic British Cars

Abbeydale Press

1903 Humberette

1926 MG 14/28

1964 Aston Martin DB5

This revised and updated paperback edition printed in 2007

ISBN 978-1-86147-193-2

1 3 5 7 9 10 8 6 4 2

Published by Abbeydale Press
An imprint of Bookmart Limited
Blaby Road, Wigston
Leicestershire, LE18 4SE
England

Cover design: Omnipress Ltd

Photographic Credits
The majority of images have been supplied from the photographic library of the National Motor Museum at Beaulieu. We are indebted to the librarian, Jonathon Day, for his help in compiling this book. The photographs appearing on pages 64-5, 166, 172-3, 174-5 and 186-7 were kindly supplied by the author Graham Robson.

Originally published in 2000 by Bookmart Limited
as *Classic British Cars*

Printed in Thailand

Below: 1948 Jaguar XK120

Title page: 1937 Lagonda V12

Contents

Foreword

It was Herbert Austin who said 'I make motor cars for the man in the street'. He was referring, of course, at the time to the Austin Seven. Motoring and the motor car have changed so much in the last 115 years, as initially, only the wealthy could afford a car. A little unfairly, the automobile has often been referred to as the plaything of the rich.

The 1920s and 1930s, brought motoring within the reach of more people and in the process, changed the landscape. It produced bigger and better roads, roadside garages and cafes, and above all a change in the architecture of the urban landscape. There was ribbon development and the arrival of the integral garage which was to change the shape of all houses. Now, a high proportion of the population either own a car or have access to one.

One of the most difficult jobs for a curator or director of a motor museum, is the choice of vehicles to put on display to the visitor. Certainly at Beaulieu we are continually refining the collection, rather than adding to it, as space is always at a premium. I had a similar dilemma when selecting cars to feature in this book. In choosing cars from the earliest to the latest, I ultimately opted for the more popular models; I was determined, however, to be a little unpredictable so you will find examples of the obscure and some of the less well-designed.

Probably the most difficult selection was vehicles to appear in the modern classic section. When choosing vehicles for the National Motor Museum's collection, we like at least twenty years of hindsight!

Michael E. Ware
Director, National Motor Museum, Beaulieu, England

1903 Wolseley Horizontal Twin

1993 McLaren F1

Veteran Era

1896–1914

Arnold-Benz ✪ Arrol-Johnston Dogcart
Daimler 4 hp (twin) ✪ Wolseley Horizontal Twin
Humberette ✪ Alldays & Onions 10/12
Vauxhall 6 ✪ Lagonda Tricar
Rolls-Royce 40/50 hp Silver Ghost
Napier 60 hp 'Six' ✪ Ford Model T
Lanchester 38 hp ✪ Argyll 25 hp

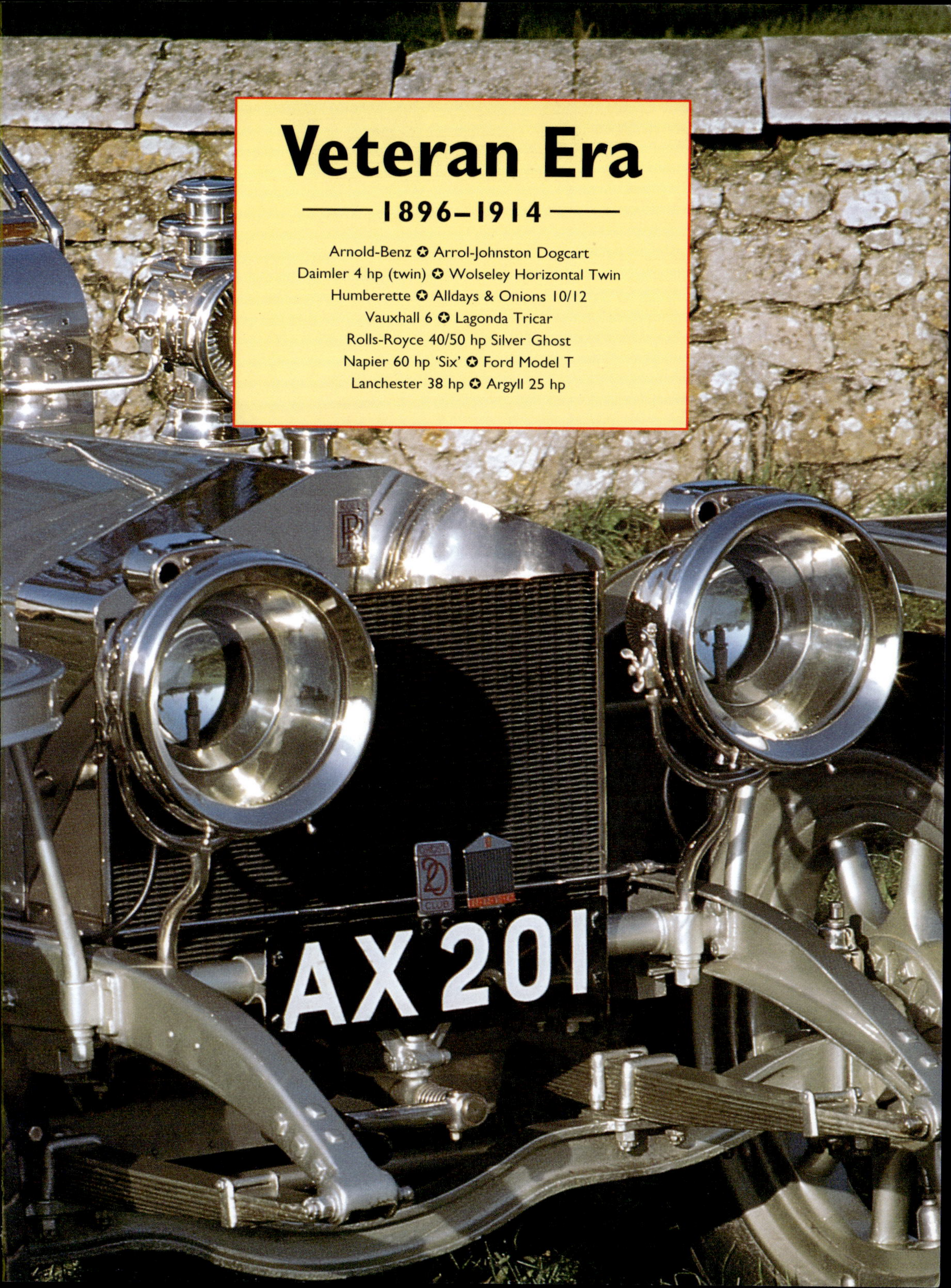

Veteran Era

Although a number of British motor cars can be counted among the 'greats' of the 20th century, Great Britain was not actually a motoring pioneer. The world's first cars were built in Germany, where Nicolaus Otto designed the first practical petrol-driven engine, and where Benz and Daimler made the first practical 'horse-less carriages'. It was in France, however, that a fledgling motor industry was first founded. Panhard & Levassor and Peugeot were soon joined by De Dion Bouton, after which expansion was swift. Both France and Germany were well ahead of Britain, and although the Americans started late, they soon overwhelmed everyone with their low-cost/mass-production expertise.

Although steam-driven monstrosities had been tried on British roads in the early part of the nineteenth century, horse-drawn machinery (particularly the personal carriage, and the stagecoach) was not easy to dislodge. Petrol-driven cars were not really established until the late 1890s. This was not through lack of interest from forward-looking individuals, but because of official legal obstruction to such machinery, which were classified as 'light locomotives' according to legislation passed in 1865 and 1878. At that point, all such vehicles were limited to speeds of two mph in towns, and to four mph in the countryside, and had to be attended by three persons. Originally, an attendant walking ahead of the 'locomotive' was obliged to carry a red flag as a warning to nervous horse owners, but this requirement was dropped in 1878.

Society was slow to embrace the technological advances heralded by the motor car, partly because the vested interest of much of the Establishment rested either in railway travel or in the huge industry surrounding horse-drawn transport – farriers, ostlers, breeders, traders and carriage makers. It was only after spirited lobbying and ridicule from the first few motorists who had imported cars from Germany or France, that the 'Locomotives on Highways', or 'Emancipation Act' came into force in 1896, which freed vehicles under 1.5 tons (1,524 kg) of all restrictions, and permitted them to travel at speeds up to a sensational 12 mph. The original London-Brighton run of November 1896 was held to celebrate this great achievement.

Right: At the turn of the century, cars were expensive and invariably driven by the rich – as the size of the houses in the background of this 1899 photograph of the Holloway brothers (front) and passenger Warwick Wright (back) in their Daimler 4 hp Twin confirms.

Opposite page: The Emancipation Run. Walter Arnold driving one of his Arnold cars from London to Brighton, in November 1896, was celebrating the increase of highway speed limits to 12 mph.

That speed limit, incidentally, would rise to 20 mph in 1903 (a speed which few cars could then achieve, never mind exceed). The speed limit was not changed, however, until 1930, by which time it was being widely ignored, in spite of ruthless policing (by speed trap) from local police forces.

BRITISH PIONEERS

While European cars dominated the market of the 1890s, one or two British inventors had worked to produce prototypes. Bremer's four-wheeler of 1894 was an unconvincing pram-like affair which never achieved reliability (or even went on sale), while the Knight (originally a three-wheeler) and the Petter of 1895 were more practical.

By 1896 in Birmingham the Lanchester brothers and Herbert Austin (for Wolseley) had both built commendably advanced prototypes, while Walter Arnold had built a dozen or so Benz machines, but Britain's first series-production motor car was the Daimler, which went on sale later in that year. Assembled at a converted cotton mill in Coventry, in a business run by company promoter Harry Lawson (who later went to jail for a variety of financial frauds), this was a surprisingly good car to emerge from a very shadily-financed concern. At first no more than an accurate license-built copy of the latest German Daimler models, this car gradually evolved, and from the early 1900s would not only be independent, but would have an altogether more respectable background.

Over the next few years there was a rush to mechanise Great Britain, first with motor cycles, then tricycles, and eventually with four-wheeler cars. Attend any old-machine event today, and you will see Rover and Singer cycles, Triumph motor cycles and Lagonda tricars, all of which confirm these trends.

By the mid-1900s British cars were not yet available in abundance, but they had become surprisingly reliable. Daimler and Lanchester had been joined by Rolls-Royce, Napier, Riley, Rover, Humber, Sunbeam and other more ephemeral makes, though at this stage all cars were essentially hand-built, hand-crafted, and expensive. In the early years of the century, cars in Britain were invariably owned by rich men with large houses or country estates; they garaged their new automobiles in motor houses once used to stable the horses and their carriages, and employed driver/mechanics (chauffeurs) to drive them around. Price was considered less important than style, presence and dependability – and since almost every car was faster than a trotting horse, a lack of performance was not critical at first. This not only explains why it took years for cheap and simple cars to be developed, but also why there was a sudden plethora of magnificent marques from which to choose. In the early years of the century Napier led, Daimler struggled valiantly to follow, and Rolls-Royce almost immediately joined in.

The first Napiers, from a long-established London company, were big, fast, impressive, and soon had an enviable motor racing reputation. Through their principal engineer/manager, S.F. Edge, they were always placed at the cutting edge of publicity, especially when they became the first to use a six-cylinder engine.

Daimler, unwilling to join such a competitive battle for motor racing supremacy, went for high style and elegant furnishings, along with high-tech engineering instead, and introduced a sophisticated series of double sleeve-valved engines from 1909. By this time they had also secured royal patronage, and therefore became the make of car which typified the gentry who bought them. Who needed advertising, when the list of owners included royal highnesses, dukes, earls and their descendants?

This, therefore, is the right moment to introduce Rolls-Royce, a company which started quietly in a back street of Manchester, but blossomed in 1906 after the introduction of the immortal 40/50 hp Silver Ghost, and shortly moved to a new factory in Derby. With this single model (there would be no other until the early 1920s), Henry Royce established a legend, and although it took decades for British royalty to take Rolls-Royce to their hearts, by 1914 they were recognised as the 'Best Cars in the World' – a phrase which the company itself was always happy to use in its promotional material.

By 1910, in fact, the British motor industry was well established, for not only had Lanchester and Rover started building sturdy, middle class machinery, but they had been joined by marques like Sunbeam of Wolverhampton (the noted engineer Louis Coatalen joined them from Hillman in 1909), and Talbot, which was already building cars in London's North Kensington. Cars were also being built north of the Border, in Scotland: by Argyll (whose new factory at Alexandria, near Loch Lomond, was a positive palace by previous standards) and Arrol-Johnston, which built cars in Paisley from 1906, but then moved, with great enterprise, to Dumfries in 1913.

Production of British cars built up steadily at this time, but it was clear to every tycoon that prices would have to be driven down considerably before Britain's burgeoning middle classes could join in the fun. One type of car which was still virtually unknown, not only here but in Europe, was the sports car. Cynics might say that because of their mechanical fragility and their character, every early car was a sports car, but this ignores the fact that sports cars should have two seats, open-top styling, and sparkling performance. Vauxhall's very rare 'Prince Henry', and one or two highly-priced Napiers qualified, but there would be none in numbers until the 1920s.

BIG HITTERS

None of Britain's 'big six' – the car makers whose cars flooded our roads from the 1930s to the 1960s – were among the pioneers, though once established, all of them soon took up dominant positions. Standard of Coventry was set up first in 1903 with a modest single-cylinder-engined machine, but would not become major producers until the 1920s.

Vauxhall, originally at Lambeth, in London, was founded in the same year, and made 76 cars in 1904, but made no real progress until the business relocated to Luton in 1905. Only a few years later, under a charismatic new chief engineer, L.H. Pomeroy (Senior), their sports cars and racing cars were among the best: true fame and serious production would come in the 1920s, not only because of the excellence of the 30/98 sports car, but because of Vauxhall's take-over by General Motors of the USA.

Opposite page: The chauffeur, clad in driving uniform complete with goggles, allows the proud owner to pose behind the wheel of his new Austin in this 1907 photograph taken outside Belvoir House in Fareham, Hampshire, while family and friends admire the car.

Left: This 1902 10 hp Wolseley was designed by Herbert Austin who later went on to start his own company in 1906. The Austin name was to play a significant part in British car manufacturing throughout the 20th century.

Austin, too, started modestly in 1906, though their founder, Herbert Austin, was already noted for his design work at Wolseley. Solidly established by 1914, huge expansion followed in the 1920s.

Hillman was set up in Coventry by William Hillman in 1907, but although this company built solid, middle class cars until the 1920s, it was not until they were forced into a merger with their next-door neighbour Humber in 1928 (both later being subsumed into the Rootes Group) that the size of the company began to matter.

The two biggest hitters of all – Ford and Morris – did not even get started in England until just before the First World War. Ford, of course, was an American firm, which had been in business since the end of the previous century, but true quantity production did not begin until the now-legendary Model T was announced in 1908. Henry Ford was finally persuaded to set up an assembly operation, for Model Ts, at a factory in Trafford Park, Manchester. As expected, he did nothing by halves, and this facility soon out-shone anything so far achieved by British nationals.

Although the Model T was incredibly cheap, and sold fast in the UK, its potential was always hampered by the annual car licence fee exacted on British cars, which favoured small-engined cars with tiny piston area: the 2.9-litre Model T had neither, and suffered. Even so, until the Bullnose Morris hit the market in numbers, the T was Britain's best-selling car.

Morris, which started production in 1913, was the last of the 'big six' to start work, and made little impact in this period. William Morris began in tiny premises with what is called an 'assembled car' (where the parent factory built almost nothing of its own, but merely screwed together components supplied by outside specialists), and very few facilities. Although Morris became Britain's best-selling car-maker in the mid 1920s, only 1,300 Morrises were produced in 1913, all of them Bullnose Oxfords, and the company's original market share was a mere 3.8 per cent.

By 1914, when the motor car had still only been legally approved for use on British roads for 18 years, annual production had risen to at least 34,000 cars. Until the late 1900s, horses and their carriages still outnumbered cars on British roads (particularly outside major towns and cities), but after that the motor car took precedence. The last pre-war British Motor Show was held at London's Olympia in 1913, when no fewer than 211 makes (from ten countries) were listed in *The Autocar's Buyers' Guide*. By the time the outbreak of war put paid to private car production in 1914, more than 130,000 cars (almost all British) were already on the roads, which themselves had changed immeasurably in just two decades.

But if such figures sounded impressive, what followed in the 1920s and 1930s would dwarf them all. At the turn of the century, motoring had been strictly for the rich, and by 1914 it was for the merely 'well-to-do'. By 1930 'motoring for the masses' would have arrived.

1896 Arnold-Benz

Britain's motor industry did not exist in 1894, not only because the motor car itself was new and rare, but because British legislation still discouraged its use. It was not until pioneers like Walter Arnold & Sons (of Kent) took the plunge that any sort of domestic manufacture took place.

In 1894 Walter Arnold imported a 1.5-litre Benz from Germany, believing that the climate for motoring must soon change, and that there was a market for the new-fangled 'horse-less carriages' in the UK. He agreed with Benz to produce a British version of the car. The first customer car was sold before the 1896 Act 'liberated' the British car, almost certainly making the Arnold-Benz the first 'British' car to go on sale.

Over in Germany, Benz was in direct competition with Daimler, whose UK branch in Coventry produced the first British-built Daimler cars from 1896. Unlike in Germany, however, the Benz-based cars did not prosper, and only a dozen machines were built and sold before Arnold abandoned its enterprise. This was not the end of the Arnold company, however, as a descendant of the concern exists in the UK today.

The very first Arnold car (an amalgam of British and German components and engineering), known as 'Adam', actually took part in the London-Brighton 'Emancipation Run' in November 1896, and is today on show in the National Motor Museum at Beaulieu. Like the Benz cars of the day, the Arnold was built around a wooden chassis frame, which was strengthened with iron flitch plates. The engine itself was an oversquare single-cylinder unit, with an atmospheric inlet valve (which opened when the cast iron piston sucked in the mixture on its induction stroke), and a gravity-fed surface carburettor.

The engine was located under the high mounted seats, driving the rear wheels through a two-speed 'fast and loose' pulley clutch, with final drive from the transmission cross-shaft by exposed chain (which had to be lubricated at least once every day). To start the engine, the flywheel was rotated by the chauffeur's gloved hand.

Like the running gear, the rest of the design was crude, with spindly wire-spoke wheels (those at the rear being much larger than the front), external-contracting brake bands at the rear, and a spoon brake on the solid rear tyre. A driver could count himself lucky if he completed a 30-mile journey (at 30 mpg fuel economy) without a breakdown of some sort. This, though, was pioneer British motoring, without which the motor car could never have progressed.

Arnold-Benz

Years in production: 1896–98
Structure: Mid/rear engine/rear-drive. Separate wooden chassis
Engine type: 1-cylinder, automatic inlet, side exhaust valve
Bore and stroke: 123.8 x 111.1 mm
Capacity: 1,190 cc
Power: 1.5 bhp @ 65 rpm
Fuel supply: Gravity fed surface carburettor
Suspension: Beam-axle front, beam-axle rear
Top speed: 16 mph

Below: Steering in the Arnold-Benz pistoned engine was by a vertical steering column and a twin open rack. Ten mph felt perilously fast in this machine, where the occupants sat up high, and totally exposed to the elements.

1898 Arrol-Johnston Dogcart

Arrol-Johnston was one of the most famous early makes of car in Scotland, and was introduced at a time when the fledgling industry looked like being an important part of Scotland's industrial fabric. This early promise soon faded, for no cars were made north of the Border after the 1920s until Rootes set up a new plant in the 1960s to manufacture Hillman Imps.

The Arrol-Johnston marque was founded very early in the life of the British motor industry, in 1897, when Sir William Arrol (the noted civil engineer) and George Johnston got together to develop the original 'Dogcart' model, which went into production in a factory at Camlachie, an industrial area of Glasgow. The city was not short of industrial skills, of course, but in the

Victorian era they had been applied mainly to heavy industries, such as shipbuilding.

A 'dogcart' was a particularly compact style of horse-drawn carriage, where two rows of seats were placed back-to-back. The carriage was so small and light that, on a private estate at least, it could be drawn by a pony or a large dog! Like many 'horseless carriages', the pioneering Arrol-Johnston's style was lifted from the earlier era, though in this case the solid-tyred wheels were altogether larger, and the flat-twin opposed-piston engine was positioned under the floor, driving the rear wheels by chain.

Above: The flat-twin pistoned engine was positioned under the floor, driving the rear wheels by chain, but its performance was limited.

Although the performance was distinctly limited (and, even then, it was beginning to look old-fashioned), this was such a strong, reliable, popular and practical layout that it was produced, with only minor changes, until 1907, by which time a more modern front-engined 12/15 model had appeared.

The brakes were arranged in the form of shoes which could be pressed on the back of the solid rear tyres – not very effective in dry weather, and virtually useless when it was raining. The suspension, on the other hand, was relatively comfortable, for there were full elliptic leaf springs at the front, and half-elliptics at the rear. Transmission and brake control levers were mounted close to the driver's right hand, and some cars were fitted with magnificent bulb horns.

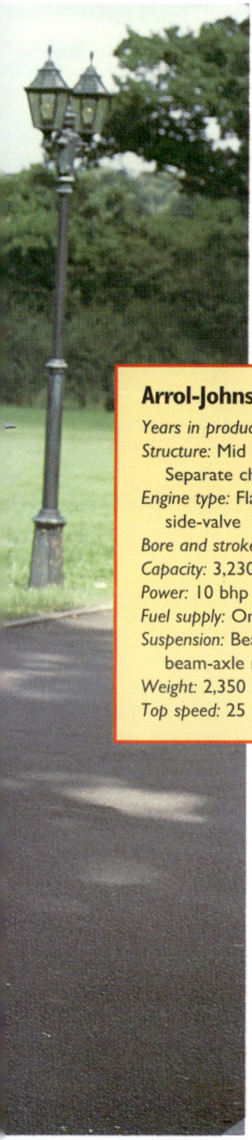

Arrol-Johnston Dogcart

Years in production: 1898–1907
Structure: Mid engine/rear-drive Separate chassis
Engine type: Flat-2 cylinder, side-valve
Bore and stroke: 100 x 86.4 mm
Capacity: 3,230 cc
Power: 10 bhp @ unstated rpm
Fuel supply: One carburettor
Suspension: Beam-axle front, beam-axle rear
Weight: 2,350 lb
Top speed: 25 mph

This was a good foundation for the marque, which prospered into the 1910s and 1920s but, like many other companies, suffered badly from the arrival of cheaper, series-production machinery made in the Midlands. In spite of a move to Dumfries in 1913, and a merger with Aster (of Wembley, Middlesex) in 1927, the pedigree fell away, the last of all being produced in 1931.

Left and right: The Dogcart's layout owed as much to the past, as to the future – the large wheels were constructed from wood, there was no weather protection for the passengers, and the brakes were virtually non-existent.

1899 Daimler 12 hp

Although Daimler, of Coventry, was one of the very first British manufacturers to make and sell motor cars in any numbers, for the first few years it had to rely on license-built designs from the Daimler company of Germany. Even so, starting from premises in a converted textile mill, it soon built up its business, and began producing all-British models in the early 1900s.

The original Daimler, started life as the invention of Gottlieb Daimler, of Cannstatt, whose pioneering 'horseless carriage' had gone on the road in 1886. After producing internal combustion engines for sale to other concerns, Daimler began building cars in 1896. A licence to build these twin-cylinder engined cars in Britain was taken out by one Harry Lawson, a vigorous promoter of car businesses, whose intention seems to have been to corner the market. Using fair means and foul, he failed in this, and spent time in jail as a result, but the Daimler marque prospered.

Looking back with a century's hindsight, one could say that the first Daimlers were almost impossibly crude and spidery in the extreme, but we must also remember that they were among the first reliable machines which did not require horses, oxen or human power to move them down the roads. Without previous experience on which to draw, these 'horseless carriages' were just that – developments of carriages which might once have been pulled by horses, but now had a petrol engine mounted underneath the frame instead.

With a top speed of no more than 15-20 mph, and a cruising speed (if anything so chancy or restless can be described in this way) of no more than 10 mph, features such as suspension and braking could be virtually ignored, handling meant nothing, and it was the fight for reliability which was paramount. The 12 hp model which followed in 1899 was altogether more sophisticated, for it had a more powerful four-cylinder engine in the nose. Described by *The Motor Car Journal* as 'the most up-to-date carriage built in this country', in

Daimler 12 hp

Years in production: 1899–1903
Structure: Front-engine/rear-drive. Separate chassis
Engine type: 4-cylinder, automatic inlet valve
Bore and stroke: 90 x 120 mm
Capacity: 3,054 cc
Power: 12 bhp @ unspecified rpm
Fuel supply: Spray-type carburettor
Suspension: Beam-axle front, beam-axle rear
Weight: Not quoted
Top speed: 25 mph (approx.)

July 1899 the Hon. John Scott-Montagu's car (which is illustrated) was the first-ever petrol-engined vehicle to enter the precincts of the Houses of Parliament.

Like many cars of its day, this machine has a front-mounted engine, a gearbox under the seats, and final drive to the rear wheels was by chain. Although pneumatic tyres were fitted to the front wheels, early examples had solid rear tyres.

Although the styling of late-Victorian cars differs completely from those of today, their mechanical layout was already edging towards what became an industry standard for many decades to come.

Above: A choice of body styles was available, and during the four-year life of this machine a number of subtle improvements were made to the specification. Early cars had near-vertical steering columns, though a more raked wheel was added later.

1903 Wolseley Horizontal Twin

The Wolseleys of 1900–1905, which were actually designed by Herbert Austin (who would later found his own car-making concern), were the first wholly British cars to be mass-produced. (Earlier cars like the Victorian Daimlers were inspired by Daimler-Benz cars from Germany). Prototype Wolseleys were the pioneering tricars of 1896 and 1898, and the first four-wheeler voiturette followed in 1899. Examples of the four-wheeler competed successfully in the Automobile Club's 1000 Miles trial of 1900, after which series production began in Birmingham.

The first Wolseley actually to go on sale was a single-cylinder model, which was speedily followed by others: twins and horizontally-aligned flat-four cylinder types, all with similar cylinder dimensions and valve gear details, and the same simple type of chassis and transmission.

Although the engines were physically large, they were not, of course, very powerful. They were located under the front of the chassis, ahead and under the toe-board, with cooling radiators and accessories above them, and a chain-driven final drive to the rear axle, which, with the exception of the French Système Panhard was the accepted layout of the period.

Cylinder heads pointed forwards, towards the nose of the car, which helped to keep them cool. The first twin-cylinder Wolseley arrived in 1901, and was effectively a doubling up of the original single-cylinder power unit, eventually pushing out a creditable 12 bhp. The early cars used an 'automatic' or 'atmospheric' inlet valve in their engines, which was opened by suction when the cylinder drew in fuel/air mixture, and which was forced back on to its seat by compression and combustion. This was inefficient, and was supplanted by a mechanically-operated inlet valve on later types. The transmission was complex – a Renolds chain drove from the clutch to a separate mid-mounted transmission, then through a four-speed gearbox, with twin chain drives to the rear wheels from the mid-mounted gearbox counter shaft, all the chains requiring regular (daily, ideally) attention and oiling.

The development of these cars came to an abrupt end in 1905, when Wolseley's directors wanted to see new vertical engine models introduced. Herbert Austin refused to carry out their wishes and therefore walked out, but this might just have been a good excuse, as the original Austin-badged cars, which followed within a year, had vertical engines.

The last horizontal-engined Wolseley was built in 1906, and a series of more conventional, Siddeley-inspired cars succeeded them.

Wolseley Horizontal Twin

Years in production: 1901–05
Structure: Front engine/rear-drive Separate chassis
Engine type: Flat 2-cylinder, over-head inlet-valve/side-exhaust valve
Bore and stroke: 114.3 x 127 mm
Capacity: 2,606 cc
Power: 10 bhp @ 700 rpm
Fuel supply: One Wolseley carburettor
Suspension: Beam-axle front, beam-axle rear
Weight: 2,130 lb
Top speed: 20 mph

Left: No fewer than 327 of all types were sold in 1901, rising to 800 in 1903. At the time this made Wolseley the most prolific of all British makes, a lead which it retained until the outbreak of the First World War a decade later.

1903 Humberette

If you are a lover of Classic (rather than Veteran) cars, you probably remember a Humber as a large, ponderous but well equipped member of the Rootes Group. If you are a vintage enthusiast, you will no doubt remember the famous 8/18s, 12/25s and 14/40s of the 1920s. But this is to forget the origins of Humber, which are in the 1890s, in Beeston, Nottingham.

Humber (like many other marques) evolved from a company which had originally made pedal cycles (for Nottingham had a thriving bicycle industry for much of the century). Although Beeston originally dabbled with the abortive Pennington car project, the first engine-driven, Humber-badged, machines from Beeston were motor tricycles and quadricycles, followed by tricars. The first cars had two- or four-cylinder engines, but they were succeeded by the tiny single-cylinder-engined Humberette (literally, 'small Humber'), a sturdy and well made machine with only a little power, yet the miracle was that it could carry a useful payload.

By comparison with previous Humbers, this was an ambitious project, for it featured a De Dion style of front-mounted water-cooled engine, with a leather-covered cone clutch, a two-speed gearbox controlled by levers under the steering wheel, as well as drive shaft to the rear wheels – the last being a real novelty in the early 1900s. The steering wheel, by the way, had only a single spoke, a characteristic of early Humbers, and quite 50 years ahead of the time when Citroen 're-invented' it. Braking, always a chancy business on cars of this period, was by externally contracting elements which were exposed to the weather. Even so, it was well made and (like other Beeston-Humbers) it was more substantially built and more expensive than equivalent cars from Humber's Coventry factory.

The original Humberette, while respected, was soon seen to be under-powered, so within a year the engine had been enlarged to 762 cc from 611 cc, though few cars were sold, and Humber rather dropped the idea of a 'small car' when the business was concentrated in Coventry in 1908. 'Humberette', though, was a intriguing name to use, so the company tried again in 1914, with an entirely different, larger, V-twin-engined car. In the 1920s Humber turned to building larger, more conventional cars, eventually merging with Hillman in 1928, and becoming a founder member of the Rootes Group.

Right: The original Humberette was probably the British car industry's first successful attempt to produce a popular light car, though as new-fangled motor cars still appealed mainly to the rich, it was difficult to get buyers interested.

Humberette

Years in production: 1903–08
Structure: Front engine/rear-drive Separate chassis
Engine type: 1-cylinder, automatic inlet, side exhaust valve
Bore and stroke: 92.1 x 92.1 mm
Capacity: 611 cc
Power: 5 hp
Fuel supply: Longuemare float-type carburettor
Suspension: Beam-axle front, beam-axle rear
Weight: 650 lb
Top speed: 25 mph

1904 Alldays & Onions 7 hp

Although this car's name was quaint, there was nothing strange about its engineering, or its behaviour. Established in Birmingham in 1899, the company started with a single-cylinder machine. As with most such British machines, inspiration came from overseas, for this 'Traveller' was merely a quadricycle with a French de Dion engine.

The company did not really make its name until 1905, when the original own-design twin-cylinder 10/12 went on sale. Although this was a major new undertaking, Alldays was confident of success. The general feeling in the company, and throughout Birmingham, where Britain's nascent motor industry was based, was that motor car sales were continually increasing, and that anything was possible.

The first twentieth-century Alldays & Onions model was the 7 hp of 1904, which had a modern-looking layout and style, but was powered only by a side-valve, single-cylinder, front-mounted engine. This was merely the start for the company's development, but it showed that the company already knew what would appeal to the public.

Like other early-1900s British cars, the 7 hp looked chunky and purposeful, with a sturdy frame, lofty seating positions, and a conventional chassis which included leaf-spring suspension and artillery-style wooden wheels. The original 10/12s had simple chassis frames, with artillery-style wooden wheels and pneumatic tyres (though these, alas, were by no means as puncture resistant as the makers would have liked). The engine was a water-cooled vertical twin with side-valves, and was soon renowned as a smooth, no-nonsense slogger.

Alldays were so ambitious (and self-confident) that in 1908 they absorbed the car-maker Enfield of Redditch (the same company with connections to the famous rifle and bicycle business), and developed new and more expensive cars. The 10/12 was therefore allowed to languish, and the last Alldays-badged cars were sold in 1918, for by this time the business had developed its alternative (and expensive) Enfield-Alldays range, which sold in limited numbers until 1925.

Alldays & Onions 7 hp

Years in production: 1904–08
Structure: Front engine/rear-drive. Separate chassis
Engine type: 1-cylinder, side-valve
Bore and stroke: 101.6 x 114.2 mm
Capacity: 926 cc
Power: 7 bhp at unspecified rpm
Fuel supply: Single carburettor
Suspension: Beam axle front, beam axle rear

Right: Once seen as sturdy and long-lasting, its reputation spread rapidly by word of mouth and it became one of Britain's most successful 'small' cars. It was not until the market's stability was upset by the arrival of the Morris Bullnose model, and the cheap Ford Model T, that its popularity died away.

V.C.C.
1904
ALLDAYS

1904 Vauxhall 7 hp

When the first motor cars arrived on British roads, the Vauxhall Iron Works on the south bank of the Thames was only interested in marine engineering. Its first cars were inspired by the German Benz machines though there was some evidence of American influence too, and were designed as a co-operative effort between F.W. Hodges and the official receiver of the company. Even so, they had little chance to develop the cars, or the car-making business in London, for within a year the company had run out of space. Accordingly, it up-rooted itself, to a new greenfield site at Luton, in Bedfordshire, where it remains to this day.

Although the original Vauxhall was rated at, and named, a 5 hp machine, it was the 6 hp model of 1904 which was the first to go on sale. By the standards, and sales levels, of the day, it was an immediate success and 776 vehicles were sold in the year. At a time when most car designers looked back to the standard of horse-drawn carts, one advanced feature was the use of coil springs for front and rear suspension beams.

The low-revving single cylinder engine measured 1,029 cc (as large as a small four-cylinder family car of the late 1990s), but only produced 6 horsepower, and needed a two-speed gearbox to provide a top cruising speed of 15 mph. Contemporary pictures of those early cars show a compact four-seater layout – the wheelbase was only 6 ft 9 in, (2,057 mm) the overall length not more than about 9 ft (2,743 mm). Only one year later, the company introduced a radically different model, the 7/9 hp, which not only had a three-cylinder engine, but it was mounted at the front of the car.

This became the company's staple product for more than a year, and all types had distinctive, rakish, styling, complete with a vee-nose and a front-mounted radiator. Early types has a 1.3-litre engine and 7 hp, but were underpowered, so a larger, 9 bph, 1,436 cc engine soon became a standard fitting.

Except for its engine, this model was conventional by early Edwardian standards, for it had a three-speed sliding-type gearbox behind the engine, chain drive to the rear axle, and there was a transmission brake behind the gearbox. Pneumatic tyres were usually standard, this handsome machine being available in a variety of body styles.For Vauxhall, though, this was only the beginning, as L.H. Pomeroy went on to design a series of fine Edwardian and Vintage cars, before General Motors took over the business in 1925.

Below: The 7/9 hp was Vauxhall's first multi-cylinder model, a much more conventional machine than the original type. The three-cylinder engine was mounted up front under the shapely bonnet. There was a choice of body styles.

Vauxhall 7/9

Years in production: 1904–05
Structure: Front engine/rear-drive. Separate chassis
Engine type: 3-cylinder, side-valve
Bore and stroke: 76.2 x 105 mm
Capacity: 1,435 cc
Power: 9 bhp at unspecified rpm
Fuel supply: One carburettor
Suspension: Beam-axle front, beam-axle rear
Weight: 1,350 lb (approx)
Top speed: 30 mph

1905 Lagonda Tricar

Some of the most glamorous of marques have humble origins. Lagonda, so famous in the 1970s and 1980s for its supercars, started out by building motor cycles; its first 'motor car' was actually a motorbike-derived tricar.

American Wilbur Gunn moved to Staines, south-west of London, in the 1890s, established the Lagonda company, and sold his first motor cycle in 1900. Although Gunn seems to have had no master plan to break into the motor car market, he was tempted by the rather simple process of incorporating motorcycle technology into a three-wheeler (hence 'tricar') frame. The first Lagonda tricar was apparently built in 1903 to satisfy an unsolicited order from a motor club secretary; Gunn found this process so straightforward that he decided to make more of them. Officially, therefore, the first 'production' tricar was launched in 1904, was gradually improved, and was not replaced by a more 'car-like' car until 1908.

Tricars are still seen competing in Veteran car events like the London-Brighton run. Although obviously derived from motorcycle engineering, they are sturdy and able to cope with reasonably long journeys (by early 1900s standards). Their layout, of course, was not at all

Lagonda Tricar

Years in production: 1904–07
Structure: Mid-engine/rear-drive. Tubular chassis
Engine type: 2-cylinder, automatic inlet valve/side exhaust valve
Capacity: 1,222 cc
Power: 12 bhp @ unspecified rpm
Fuel supply: One horizontal Longuemare carburettor
Suspension: Beam axle front, beam axle rear
Weight: 400 lb
Top speed: 20 mph

like the conventional cars which were soon to appear. There were two wheels up front, attached to a motor cycle-type frame with a single rear wheel; the air-cooled engine was fixed to the chassis tube between the driver/rider's legs, and the rear wheels were chain-driven. Almost all the machinery, including the transmission, was exposed to the elements, and susceptible to mud and road filth of all types.

There was no suspension of any sort on the earliest tricars, (although pneumatic tyres helped to give some resilience) as both front and rear wheels were fixed solidly to the frame, and steering, through a simple linkage, was not from a wheel, but from cycle-type handlebars.

The original tricar specification was not fixed for long, as Gunn reacted to market pressures, providing more powerful engines, and a modicum of creature comforts. Smaller, single-cylinder, or larger air-cooled or water-cooled twin-cylinder engines were available, chassis design was altered significantly, suspension was added, and the Royal Mail even bought a number of these cars, with a delivery 'bin' in place of the passenger's seat.

By 1907, the British tricar fashion had passed, and Lagonda's total output was 69 cars.

Below: Amazingly, the tricar was a two-seater with the passenger accommodated in a seat (often made of wicker) fixed ahead of the driver, ahead of the steering, and between the front wheels. If the tricar ever left the road, or made contact with any other vehicle, pedestrian or horse, it was the unprotected passenger who would act as an involuntary 'bumper' for the rest of the ensemble.

1906 Rolls-Royce 'Silver Ghost'

Henry Royce and Sir Charles Rolls joined forces to produce the very first Rolls-Royce cars in 1904. Royce (later knighted, to become Sir Henry) carried on as the company's titular head until the early 1930s, designing every part of the cars that bore his name.

The magnificent 40/50 hp model, soon nicknamed the 'Silver Ghost', appeared in 1906. In British terms, 40/50 denotes the engine type and its power rating: amazingly, in spite of its huge 7-litre engine, this was probably only 60 bhp, the huge car's top speed being a mere 50 mph.

Compared with any other contemporary car, the Silver Ghost was smooth, silent, ultra-reliable, and amazingly elegant. Around 8,000 were produced between 1906 and 1926, 1,700 coming from a subsidiary in Springfield, Massachusetts, USA. Not even a fast car by mid-1900s standards, it always behaved in a more refined and dignified, manner than any rival. With this model, Rolls-Royce established the 'Best Car in the World' tag that it would flaunt for so many years.

The car was available with a variety of splendidly-

built bodies, though Rolls-Royce never built their shells. There were two wheelbase lengths – 135.5 in or 143.5 in – all cars carrying the same long bonnet and patrician radiator, which had been modelled on the very best in Greek architecture. A really well-equipped limousine with up to seven seats would be driven by a chauffeur, and could weigh up to 5,000 lb. Progress was stately, rather than spirited.

The engine, conventionally laid out, had rocking levers placed between the side-mounted camshaft and the valve stems themselves. With a sturdy crankshaft, which defied the very thought of torsional vibrations, it ran silently at all times. It was quite possible to stand alongside an idling Silver Ghost and not realise that the engine was running.

Rolls-Royce Silver Ghost

Years in production: 1906–1926
Structure: Front engine/rear-drive. Separate chassis
Engine type: Six cyl, side-valve
Bore and stroke: 114.3 x 114.3 mm
Capacity: 7,036 cc
Power: Not quoted
Fuel supply: Rolls-Royce/Krebs carburettor
Suspension: Beam axle front, beam axle rear
Weight: Up to 5,000 lb

The engine itself was enlarged, to 7,428 cc, in 1909. The original gearbox, an 'overdrive' four-speed design, was replaced by a three-speeder from 1909 to 1913, after which a direct-top four-speed box was adopted.

The original platform-type of leaf-spring rear suspension gave way to conventional leaf springs at an early stage, then to a cantilever layout from 1912.

Other changes included the fitment of a spiral-bevel instead of a straight-bevel rear axle (1923), an engine torsional damper (1911), a dynamo (1919 – instead of a magneto), four-wheel brakes with a Hispano-Suiza type of servo (1924), Hartford suspension dampers (1924) and wire spoke wheels (standard from 1913).

Although the Silver Ghost was never a technological advance, Rolls-Royce ensured that it was always the world's best built and equipped machine. Approved coachbuilders gradually modernised, along graceful lines. A Silver Ghost was instantly recognisable, dignified and suitable for every occasion.

Every owner, Rolls-Royce thought, needed to employ a full-time chauffeur, trained by Rolls-Royce, someone who usually lived in the grounds of his master's house, perhaps over the garage, where there would be a fully-equipped workshop.

When the time came to retire the Silver Ghost, it needed to be replaced by a superb new model, which is why the new Phantom I did not appear until 1926.

Above and left: The huge 7-litre engine had rocking levers and a sturdy crankshaft which ran silently at all times. This was a smooth, ultra-reliable and elegant car whose progress was stately, rather than spirited.

1907 Napier 60 hp 'Six'

With a little more luck, and perhaps a little less hype, Napier might have beaten Rolls-Royce in the British prestige car stakes. Although the two marques fought, head-to-head, until the end of the 1900s, Napier then fell away.

It all began when the cycling and motorcycling pioneer Selwyn F. Edge joined the company in 1900, and became Napier's sole distributor, racing personality and arch-publicist. The first true Napier began as an engine conversion in Montague Napier's own Panhard, producing the car in which Edge competed so successfully in the Thousand Miles trial of 1900.

Early production Napiers were twin-cylinder-engined machines, a four-cylinder type followed almost at once, and the first monstrous racing types followed in 1901. By the time Edge himself had won the Gordon Bennett Cup in 1902, and a new factory had been built in Acton, west London, Napier was on the world map. Edge persuaded Montague Napier that it should build a straight-six-cylinder model, and the Type L49 of 1904 was the world's first successful example of that type. Convinced, Napier developed a whole series of magnificent 'sixes',

1907 Napier 60 hp 'Six'

Years in production: 1905–10
Structure: Front engine/rear-drive. Separate chassis
Engine type: Six-cyl., side-valve
Bore and stroke: 127 x 101.6 mm
Capacity: 7,676 cc
Power: Not stated
Fuel supply: Single Napier carburettor
Suspension: Beam-axle front, beam-axle rear
Weight: Up to 4,500 lb (depen dent on body fitted)
Top speed: 60 mph

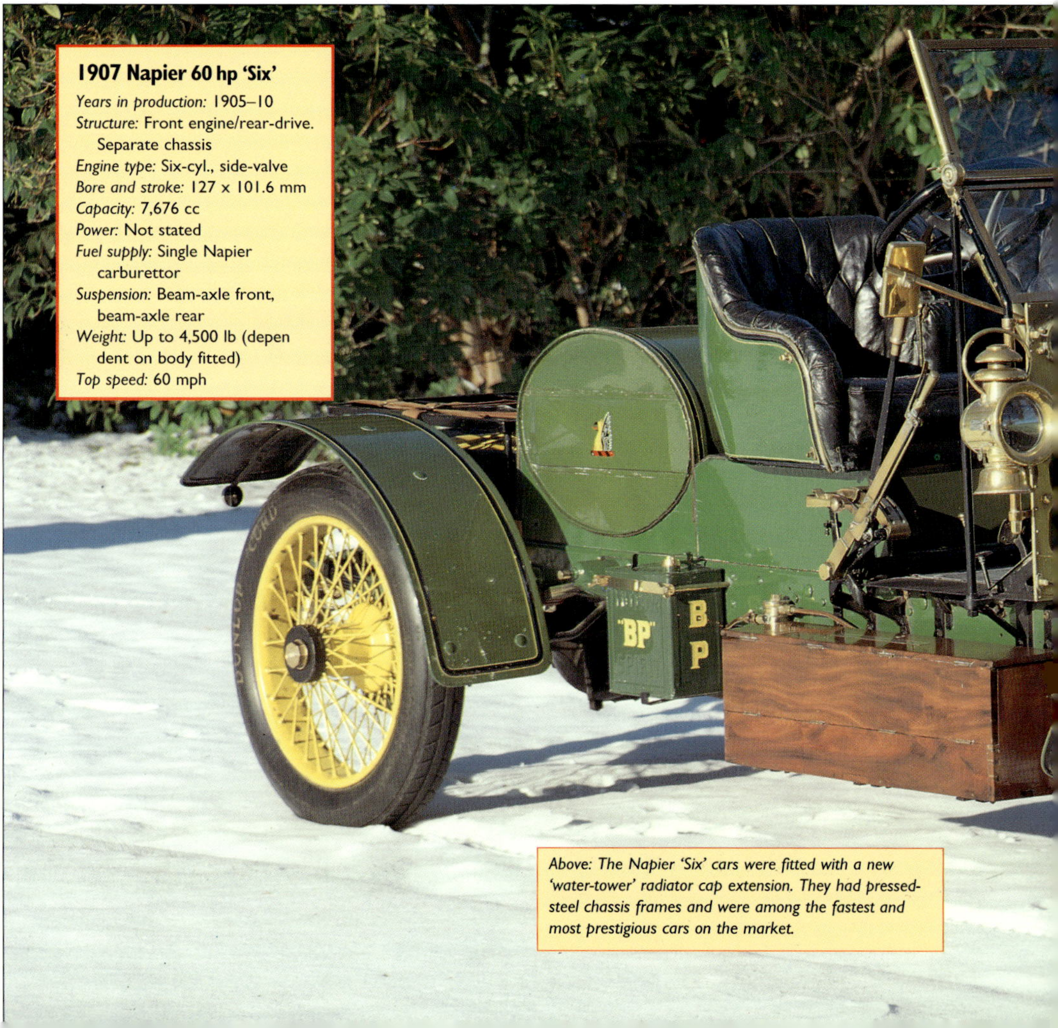

Above: The Napier 'Six' cars were fitted with a new 'water-tower' radiator cap extension. They had pressed-steel chassis frames and were among the fastest and most prestigious cars on the market.

culminating in the rare circuit racing types with engines of up to 12 litres.

The 60 hp model of 1905–10 was typical, and had a 7.7-litre side-valve engine. (Each cylinder displaced 1,279 cc, which was larger than the entire engine of the first Bullnose Morris, which would shortly arrive.) This was the third variety of Napier's 'sixes', and there would be several more in the following decade.

By later standards, of course, we would not call such a car smooth and silent, though by comparison with its contemporaries, it seemed to be so. Fitted with a distinctive new 'water-tower' radiator cap extension, a pressed-steel chassis frame, and a choice of magnificent formal coachwork, they were among the fastest, most costly, and most prestigious British cars on the market.

By 1908, Napier were offering a plethora of 'sixes' – the 4.9-litre '30' and '40', the 6.1-litre '45', the 7.7-litre '60', and the 9.7-litre '65'. They all used variants of the same Edge-inspired side-valve engine, most of them with shaft drive, and only with rear brakes; there was also a vast 15-litre '90' for which a colossal £2,500 was asked for the chassis alone. After balancing power against grace, style against practicality, the '60' was usually seen as the most desirable of all.

By the early 1910s Napier was offering far too many models from a factory which never built more than 800 cars in a year, and was overtaken in the prestige stakes by the Rolls-Royce 40/50 hp Silver Ghost. S.F. Edge moved on in 1912, and Napier's reputation was never as high again.

1908 Ford Model T

Although the world famous Ford Model T was not designed in the UK, it was assembled in this country from 1911 to 1927, and was a best-seller for many years. Here, as in the USA and the rest of the world, the Model T re-wrote the motoring script: more than 15 million were produced in the USA, and well over 250,000 were produced at a British factory at Trafford Park, on the outskirts of Manchester.

Henry Ford's first car, the Quadricycle prototype, was finished in 1896, and other Ford production cars followed it, before the all-new Model T appeared in 1908. Designed from the outset to be built in huge numbers, its price fell as production rose.

Although thoughtfully equipped with a large-capacity (2.9-litre) side-valve engine, which produced lots of torque, if not much power, this was a positive disadvantage in the UK, where cars were taxed according to a formula which penalised those with considerable piston area. In spite of its complexities (an epicyclic transmission), and its crudities (an archaic chassis design, with transverse leaf front and rear springing), the Model T was so well serviced by a vast dealer chain, and so easy to fix when it did go wrong, that it immediately found a market.

Although only 10,000 cars were produced in the USA in 1909, no fewer than two million were produced at peak, in 1923. Yet, in spite of this, the Model T changed little mechanically in 20 years, only the multi-farious body styles were updated, from time to time, to represent progress.

The chassis itself was definitely more flexible than some of its competitors, though this, along with the transverse leaf suspension and big wheels, made it possible to pick one's way over the sometimes poor road surfaces of the 1910s and 1920s. The engine was low-revving, but almost totally reliable, while the transmission had only two forward gears, changes being effected by a clutch pedal which was really a 'gear change' pedal. There was no foot accelerator pedal, for engine speed changes were produced

by moving hand levers under the steering wheel which covered throttle opening and ignition advance.

The Model T's low price (less than £250, even at peak, in the 1920s), low running costs, and reliability ensured its sales (7,000 alone in 1915), but the high annual tax (and stiff competition from the Bullnose Morris) eventually killed it off. Ford replaced it with the more conventional Model A in 1928, and were not to be as adventurous again.

Below and left: Idiosyncratic and very popular, it soon acquired nicknames, of which 'Tin Lizzie' was the most memorable. Popular songs like 'Get out and Get Under' followed, and cemented the car's reputation forever.

Ford Model T

Years in production: 1908–27
Structure: Front engine/rear-drive Separate chassis
Engine type: 4-cylinder, side-valve
Bore and stroke: 95.2 x 101.6 mm
Capacity: 2,896 cc
Power: 20 bhp @ 1,600 rpm
Fuel supply: One Holley or Kingston carburettor
Suspension: Beam-axle front, beam-axle rear
Weight: 1,450 lb
Top speed: 45 mph

1911 Lanchester 38 hp

Although Frederick Lanchester designed one of the first (and, for its day, highly advanced) British cars in 1895, his Birmingham-based company was rather slow to get its products into production. Once established in the early 20th century, Lanchester gained a reputation second only to Rolls-Royce, moving smoothly from making twin-cylinder (1901) to four-cylinder cars (1904), and to the first stately six-cylinder machines in 1906, these last having overhead-valve engines of a unique layout.

The main feature of all Frederick Lanchester's production cars was the position of the engine, which was much further back in the chassis than on later conventional machines. Although it was not fair to call a Lanchester 'mid-engined', there was certainly no long snout up front, and front seat passengers usually sat on either side of the engine, which was made as narrow as possible for that reason.

The layout of the 1911 38 hp 'six' (which was revealed at the same time as a smaller, 25 hp 'four' with a similar engine), was typical, although it would be the last of the line. Several varieties were available, and the general style of the cars exhibited a large and spacious passenger compartment, (which was always Lanchester's intention) with a surprisingly short bonnet. Even then the radiator was behind the centre line of the front wheels. This was, however, the first Lanchester to be designed by George, rather than 'Dr Fred', and it signalled a partial change towards a more conventional layout: that change would not be completed until the arrival of the later, 'Sporting Forty' of 1914.

Like earlier Lanchesters, the 38 hp had an engine with horizontal (instead of vertical) overhead-valve, ante-chamber combustion space, and the famous Lanchester wick-type carburettor. Although transmission was still by Lanchester-patented three-speed epicyclic control, it had a conventional clutch pedal and gate-type lever control.

Although this was a fine car, it was the last of that particular line. Production of both six-cylinder and four-cylinder types carried on to 1914, when work for the war effort took precedence, but they were dropped in favour of new machinery thereafter.

Lanchester retained its independence until 1931, when it was taken over by the BSA/Daimler Group. Later Lanchesters, therefore, were really re-developed Daimlers.

Lanchester 38 hp

Years in production: 1911–14
Structure: Front engine/rear-drive. Separate chassis
Engine type: 6-cylinder, overhead-valve
Bore and stroke: 101 x 101 mm
Capacity: 4,856 cc
Power: 63 bhp at 2,200 rpm
Fuel supply: Lanchester wick-type
Suspension: Beam-axle front, beam-axle rear
Weight: Approx. 3,920 lb
Top speed: 65 mph

Below: Because of the forward position of the front seats, the rear seat could also be moved forward, just ahead of the line of the rear axle, ensuring a good ride for the rear occupants, not something that could be guaranteed by Lanchester's similarly-priced rivals.

1913 Argyll 25 hp

Like Arrol-Johnston, Argyll was a respected Scottish motoring pioneer and built its first Renault-based cars in Glasgow in 1899. Unhappily, its management was deluded enough to build a vast new factory in Alexandria (near Loch Lomond), which it never filled with work, and which never came remotely close to profitability. Burdened with debt (and problems with its sleeve-valve engines), Argyll closed down for the first time in 1914, and the factory turned to other products.

Daimler had been the first British concern to adopt sleeve-valve engines (which oscillated up and down between the pistons and the cylinder block walls, opening and closing inlet and exhaust ports as they did so) and by sheer application made them work well. Argyll, with fewer resources, did not.

The original sleeve-valve Argyll was the big 25 hp (25/50) model first shown in 1911, and on sale in the following year. Except for its engine, which was big, sturdy and carefully detailed both in design and finish, with its cylinder cast in pairs, the 25/50 was an otherwise conventional machine, the top of Argyll's range, and intended to sell to the prosperous who might otherwise be in the market for a Daimler, or similar prestigious motor car.

Not only did the 25/50 hp buyer get a wide choice of stylish, up-to-the-minute coachwork (most of which was erected in the factory at Alexandria), but he got a modern chassis, which included four-wheel brakes (a real innovation by 1912 standards), a quiet and flexible engine, a four-speed transmission which included a rigid torque-tube connection between the gearbox and the back axle, along with a soft and comfortable ride, and a very high level of standard equipment. If the new-fangled engine had worked well from the outset, and if there had not been expensive legal problems about the infringement of another company's patent rights, Argyll's future might have been assured. But with prices of complete cars starting at £640 (a considerable sum for 1912), sales were limited.

Argyll soon decided to apply the same technical principle to its cheaper models, some with engines as small as 1.5-litres. Sleeve-valve engines, however, did not work as well in smaller engines, and since it was those cars which were selling increasingly well in the years before the outbreak of the First World War, Argyll was at a disadvantage.

Argyll was revived as a marque after the war in the original Glasgow factory, although the magnificent 25/50 model was not part of the post-war range. Although 1.6-litre and 2.3-litre sleeve-valve engines continued to be made, but there was no further innovation after 1922, and the last Argylls were produced in 1928.

Argyll 25 hp

Years in production: 1912–14
Structure: Front engine/rear-drive. Separate chassis
Engine type: 4-cylinder, sleeve-valve
Bore and stroke: 100 x 130 mm
Capacity: 4,082 cc
Power: 50 bhp (claimed)
Fuel supply: Single carburettor
Suspension: Beam-axle front, beam-axle rear
Weight: Up to 4,500 lb (dependent on body fitted)
Top speed: 50 mph

Right: Early Argylls had conventional (by 1900s standards) engines, but from 1909 they took up the development and manufacture of sleeve-valve engines, which were quieter and technically modern, but required precise technology and manufacturing to work properly.

The radiator badge of a Model T showing the distinctive Ford logo which has been a feature of British motoring since 1908. The present-day corporate lettering still shows a remarkable resemblance to the old logo proving that Ford is only too well aware of the significant role it has played in car history.

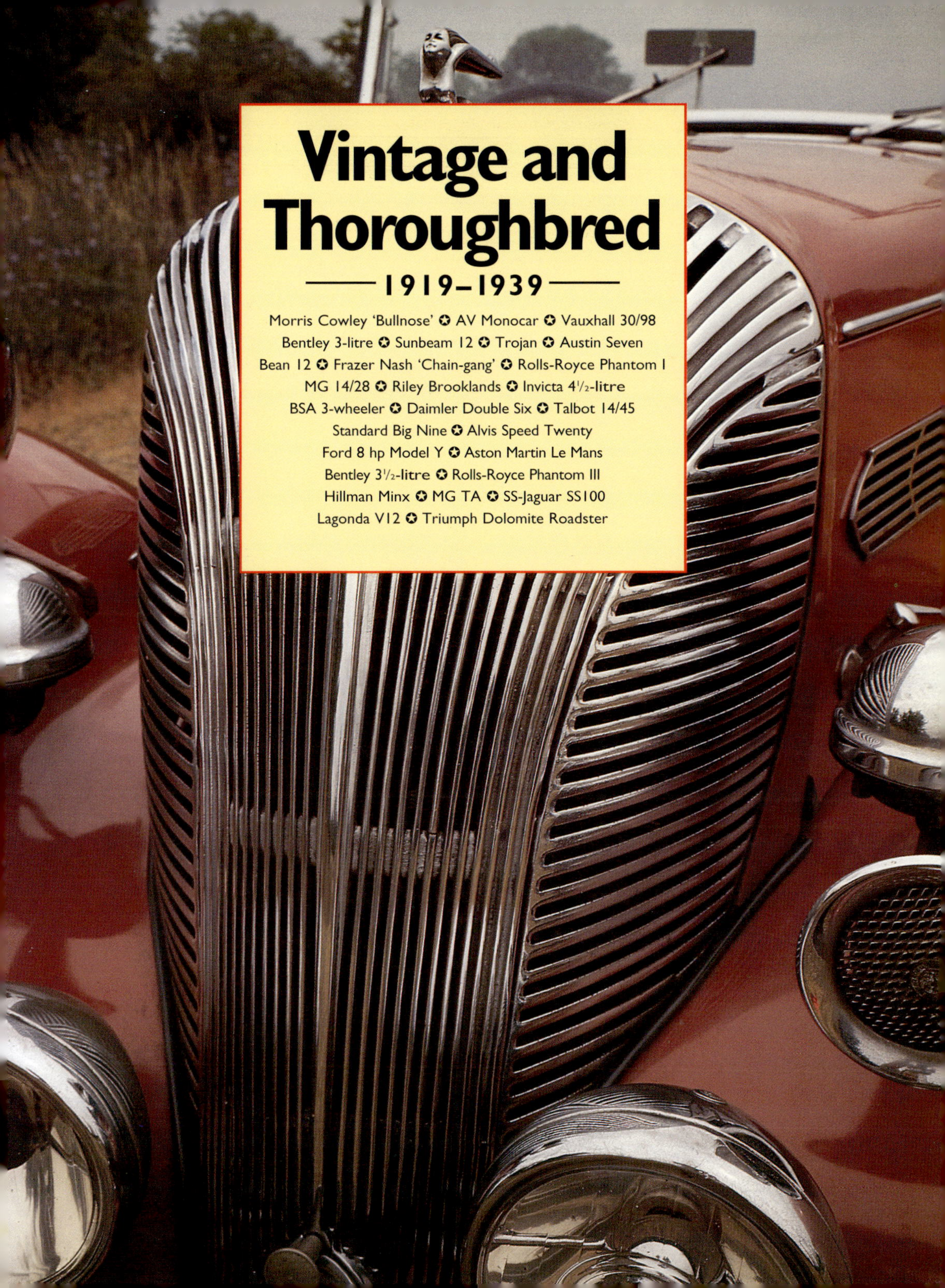

Vintage and Thoroughbred

1919–1939

Morris Cowley 'Bullnose' ✪ AV Monocar ✪ Vauxhall 30/98
Bentley 3-litre ✪ Sunbeam 12 ✪ Trojan ✪ Austin Seven
Bean 12 ✪ Frazer Nash 'Chain-gang' ✪ Rolls-Royce Phantom I
MG 14/28 ✪ Riley Brooklands ✪ Invicta 4½-litre
BSA 3-wheeler ✪ Daimler Double Six ✪ Talbot 14/45
Standard Big Nine ✪ Alvis Speed Twenty
Ford 8 hp Model Y ✪ Aston Martin Le Mans
Bentley 3½-litre ✪ Rolls-Royce Phantom III
Hillman Minx ✪ MG TA ✪ SS-Jaguar SS100
Lagonda V12 ✪ Triumph Dolomite Roadster

Vintage and Thoroughbred

Between 1919 and 1939, Britain's motor industry went through an upheaval. Recovery from the First World War was followed by the glories of what is known as the 'vintage' era, the economic traumas of the Depression of the early 1930s, and the spirited recovery which preceded the outbreak of the Second World War.

The story of this dramatic generation of motor cars must begin with a few statistics. Annual British car production shot up from 25,000 in 1919, to a peak of 341,000 in 1938, and the number of cars on the roads also exploded, from 100,000 in 1919 to just over two million in 1939. That was the good news, but the bad news was that although there were at least 100 different makes of car in production in 1919 (and many more hopeful entrants which never made it beyond the prototype stage), that figure slumped to no more than 35 in the depths of the Depression, and to a mere 32 in 1939–40. Marques which had been popular in the 1920s, such as Bean and Clyno, had disappeared by the 1930s, and marques which had been proudly independent in the 1920s found themselves taken over and transformed within ten years, a fate which befell Bentley, Sunbeam, Talbot, Lanchester and Riley, among others.

While production rose steadily during the 1920s to 170,000 cars a year, the industry, and the type of cars it produced, changed considerably. Until the mid 1920s, even mass-produced cars like the Austin Seven and the Bullnose Morris were built mainly by hand, though in a highly organised way. By the end of the decade mechanisation was sweeping in, bodies were being built from welded pressed steel panels instead of being constructed on a wooden framework, and engines were smaller.

It was only in the mid 1930s, when some die-hards (who had tired of the much cheaper, smaller and flimsier new models which had appeared) started talking of the 1920s as a 'vintage' era. Easy to define but difficult to describe, this usually meant that the cars were sturdily built, simple to maintain and often surprisingly good fun to drive.

By the 1920s a large component supply industry had been established, and engines, gearboxes and axles could be built to order, so it was possible for undercapitalised businesses to announce a new car, to rely on poorly-paid craftsmen to put them together, and to develop a reputation. Even so, of the hundreds of hopefuls who faced the 1920s in this way, few actually became established.

Below: Technological advances during the war meant that the number of cars on the roads was rapidly increasing. This 1920 photograph shows a Calthorpe with a Brooklands Hillman in the background.

THE CRâME DE LA CRâME

The best British cars of the 1920s and 1930s were produced for the comparatively small, yet excessively wealthy end of the market: some were as dignified as the Rolls-Royce Phantom and Daimler Double-Six limousines, some as fast and capable as the Bentley 8-litres and Lagonda V12s. Britain's motor cars were at the height of their fame. Big, beefy sports cars from Bentley, Invicta and Lagonda set one standard, while magnificently crafted limousines from Rolls-Royce, Daimler and (for a time) Lanchester maintained another. Although their chassis were never shatteringly modern (compared with the Germans, for instance, the British were tardy in adopting independent suspension, supercharging and V-layout engines), they were invariably well-built, and their coachwork was matchless.

Apart from the few coachbuilders who serviced the latest models from Cadillac, Packard and Duesenberg in North America, no-one could match Britain's coachbuilders. Don't believe anything you may be told about declining standards at this time – merely take a look at an H.J. Mulliner-bodied Rolls-Royce, a Hooper-bodied Daimler, and any number of sports saloons from companies like Park Ward, Gurney Nutting or Barker. 'Makes you proud to be British', was the obvious retort, which was true, as the combination of first-rate styling, a choice of tasteful trim and equipment, high quality materials, and peerless craftsmanship was unmatched. Anyone who could afford such cars – which were extremely expensive, even at 1920s and 1930s price levels – was fortunate to have so much choice.

Yet this was the high tide for such well-crafted cars. In the decades which followed, (particularly after the Second World War) social changes and soaring taxation would decimate the market. Those with an eye to the future rushed to enjoy luxury motoring while it was still practical; happily, a number of these fine cars have survived to this day.

Between 1923 and 1935, cars became much cheaper and thousands more people began driving than ever before.
Above: 1923 Triumph 10/20 hp; Top: 1935 Standard 10.

MIDDLE CLASS MOTORING

Middle class motoring came into existence during the 1920s, and took centre stage in the 1930s. As with so many of the world's innovations, once ways were found of increasing production, costs were driven down, selling prices were reduced, and the market boomed. Car makers who had annually sold dozens in the 1910s sold hundreds in the 1920s, and thousands of cars in the 1930s.

Although a typical manual worker – a factory hand, a miner, or a shipbuilder – could probably not afford a new car at this time, the white collar workers increasingly could. The professions – doctors, solicitors, architects and dentists – were first to join the ranks, followed by the middle-managers. This was a time when few could afford to pay £1,000 for a car, but thousands could afford £500; when Austin, Ford and Morris started asking less than £150 for their small-engined products, the market place exploded.

Even so, it was 'middle class' manufacturers with middle price models, who did so well in the inter-war period. By the 1930s a number of manufacturers had prospered by catering precisely for this new clientele: Alvis, Armstrong-Siddeley, Crossley, Daimler, Lanchester, Riley, Rover, SS-Jaguar, Sunbeam, Talbot, Triumph and Wolseley all competed in this keenly-fought and prestigious sector, all offering smart, well equipped cars.

The 1930s were the high point for such cars and their owners. Motoring became a middle class leisure activity: second-division coachbuilders were able to offer a great deal of visual variety in their car ranges, and magazines were produced to satisfy the curiosity of new car-owners. Advertising was surrounded by an aura of 'British is best', a complacent attitude which seemed to appeal to the motorists of the day.

SPORTY MOTORING

Among the earliest sports cars were the big, expensive Bentleys and Vauxhall 30/98s; these were followed by smaller, individualistic machines such as the Frazer Nash, and finally the small-engined two-seaters from MG, Morgan, Triumph and Singer. These vehicles, particularly those from MG, laid the foundations for the sports car boom which was to follow in the 1950s and 1960s.

There was great demand for fast small cars, if only it could be satisfied. Bentleys, Vauxhall 30/98s, twin-cam Sunbeams, Lagondas and Invictas were all extremely desirable cars, but they were also expensive, and could only be expected to sell in hundreds, not tens of thousands. Cars such as GNs and Aston Martins were great fun to drive, but prone to fall apart if abused and, as with the most expensive marques, were not backed by a large chain of dealers.

So-called sporty versions of cars like the Bullnose Morris and even the Model T Ford were simply lighter versions of the original, perhaps with the addition of unique bodywork. The breakthrough came when MG, Austin, Riley and Singer all developed truly small cars with unique frames, and tuned-engines: it was with the arrival of M-type Midgets and 9 hp Singer sports cars that demand suddenly expanded. Marques like Triumph and Lea-Francis attempted the same breakthrough, but not in the same numbers.

In only ten years MG grew from being a minor manufacturer to pre-eminence; there was a huge difference – in both engineering and in behaviour – between the Morris-based 14/28 of 1924, and the special overhead-camshaft PAs and Magnettes of 1934. Although the TA which followed was more closely based on Morris and Wolseley models than before, it was still a fine sports car. Morgan joined in, HRG appeared as a bespoke alternative and, quite suddenly, the layout of the traditional British sports car was founded.

In the meantime, the yawning gap between expensive and bargain-basement was also being filled, not necessarily with lightweight two-seaters, but with fine and stylish open models. Lovers of 1920s cars were too blinkered to

Right: Motor sport became a major source of PR for makers such as Alvis in the keenly fought battle for new customers. This photo shows the Alvis 1.5-litre team getting ready for the 1928 Le Mans Race.

Opposite page: Aston Martin, later to become a maker of prestigious cars for the top end of the market, were, in 1933, trying to satisfy the demand for small fast sports cars. This 1.5-litre model was competing in the Round Britain Rally of that year.

see the merits of many 1930s cars, which ranged from the beefy Jaguar SS100s, to two-seater Riley Sprites; from convertible Triumph Dolomite Roadsters, to the Vanden Plas-styled Alvis Speed Twenty types; from hand-built ACs, to series-production SS-Jaguar, Wolseley and Daimler models. For those in work (and, let's not forget, the effect of the Depression weighed far more heavily on the non-car-owning classes than on the middle class who could afford to buy a new car) there was far more choice of interesting and stylish machinery in the 1930s than there had been just ten years earlier.

MOTORING FOR THE MASSES

Britain's largest car makers were already established before 1914, but it was in the 1920s and 1930s that they truly came to numerical dominance. By the end of the 1920s Morris had market leadership, with Austin close behind, followed by Ford and Standard, with Humber-Hillman (the soon-to-be-named Rootes Group) and Vauxhall ready to join battle. By the end of the 1930s, Austin and Morris were more or less equal, Ford was a definite third, with the other three scrapping for 10 or 12 per cent each of the market place.

In the 1920s, the Austin Seven and the Bullnose Morris were by far the most successful cars of their type, though at the end of the period the tiny Morris Minor and the equally small Singer Junior both came close. In the early 1930s cars rated by the RAC at 8, 9, 10 and 12 hp really took over the market leadership. Every member of the 'big six' had a best-seller in this category, and though they were not technically exciting (and usually unimaginatively titled), they sold in huge numbers. Austin, of course, had the Ten, Morris had the Ten, Standard the Nine, Big Nine and, later, Flying Nine, Rootes had the ubiquitous Hillman Minx, Vauxhall the Ten-Four and Twelve-Four, while Ford swept into the market with a raft of cars all based on the original 8 hp Model Y, which became the C, evolved into the Anglia, and then spawned the Prefect.

All these cars were available as saloons, convertibles, vans, and were occasionally special-bodied, though the mass-market estate car was a type yet to be invented. Unexciting to drive (in most cases 50 mph was a good cruising speed, no more), and always likely to rot away, they were all very cheap – and motorists loved them. Thus, the scene was set for similar cars to evolve in the 1940s and 1950s.

APOCALYPSE NOW ...

If Adolf Hitler had not decided to conquer the world, the British motor industry might have evolved in a different way. By 1939, the 'big six' were embracing new technology. All-steel bodies and overhead-valve engines were almost universal, unit-construction bodies were already used by Morris, Rootes and Vauxhall, and independent front suspension had arrived at Rootes, Standard and Vauxhall. Exports were going well (nearly 80,000 in 1937), and the market was booming.

Then, at the end of the 1930s, re-armament, tax rises, the opening of aero-engined 'shadow factories' run by car makers and, from the end of 1939, a rapid conversion to military production altered the scene irrevocably. Soon Vauxhall were making tanks, Rootes were producing aircraft, Austin made trucks, while Ford constructed Merlin aero-engines. The transformation was complete: in consequence Britain's industry, and its cars, would never be the same again.

1919 Morris Cowley 'Bullnose'

The original Morris, the much-loved 'Bullnose', was Britain's equivalent – and in competition with – the Ford Model T, though its inventor, William Morris, had different ways of achieving the result. Whereas Ford had concluded that he must make as much of the car as possible in his own factories, Morris used proprietary or 'bought-in' components for some years at first.

Having started out in business by opening a cycle sales and repair shop in Oxford, Morris bought a disused building at Cowley, near Oxford (but one which adjoined open farm land), to produce cars in 1913. First with a car called the 'Oxford', then from 1915 with a smaller-engined version called 'Cowley', he built up a business which was Britain's largest car producer by 1924, when it overtook Ford UK.

The Cowley's design was as simple as that of the Model T. More conventional, it was distinguished by its rounded, bulbous, radiator style, which soon inspired the unofficial, but lasting nickname. At first almost every component was bought in, ready-manufactured, including engines from Coventry, transmissions from Birmingham, and bodies from a variety of sources. It was only as the 1920s progressed, and as the factory continued to grow, that Morris either bought up his suppliers, or started making components close to the assembly lines.

The RAC rated 'Oxford' types at 13.9 horsepower, and 'Cowley' types at 11.9 hp. They both used versions of Coventry-made engines, and many different body types were available (including super-sports versions which subsequently became the first MGs). By aggressively reducing prices at a time when costs were rising, Morris saw sales rocket.

Having produced only 3,077 cars in 1921, Morris went on to build 54,151 in 1925, by which time the Bullnose was nearly ready for replacement. As with the Model T, this market domination was achieved by cutting prices, which eventually came down to a mere £162 by 1925. No other car or model could match that, for the engines had been specifically designed to take advantage of Britain's tax laws. This, and the way that Bullnose types sold steadily throughout the countries of the Empire, ensured Morris's supremacy.

In the next few years Morris, who eventually became Lord Nuffield, allowed his business to diversify, so that far too many models were being sold at a time when the market-place was contracting, the result being that Austin rapidly caught up, and that Morris was never again as dominant as it had been in the mid 1920s.

Below: The Bullnose become a British best-seller, and Morris followed up this success by buying other marques and factories (such as Wolseley) to expand even further. His actions helped to kill off many other makes of British car which simply could not compete with Morris's tactics.

Morris Cowley 'Bullnose'

Years in production: 1915–26
Structure: Front-engine/rear-drive. Separate chassis
Engine type: 4-cylinder, side-valve
Bore and stroke: 69.5 x 102 mm
Capacity: 1,548 cc
Power: 26 bhp @ 2,800 rpm
Fuel supply: One Smith carburettor
Suspension: Beam-axle front, beam-axle rear
Weight: 1,750 lb
Top speed: 50 mph

1920 AV Monocar

Viewed from the end of the century, the AV Monocar might look like a joke, but in its day it was a popular and effective little 'cycle car'. This short-lived type of machine was really a cheap half-way house between the motor cycles and more 'grown-up' light cars of the day – and most first owners seem to have graduated to them from motor cycles when they were looking for a little more comfort, and stability. The AV was one of the first of this type, though the later, and more sporting GN became more famous.

AV of Teddington in Middlesex, was founded by Ward and Avey Ltd., who bought a cycle-car design from another struggling designer, John Carden (between 1919 and 1925 there was also a different Carden car), and began producing monocars at Carden's own factory. The first cars were delivered in 1919, and by 1922 prices had fallen to a mere £115. To make such machines profitable at those levels, they had to be more 'cycle' than substantial 'car', and were very cheaply (some say nastily) built.

As its name suggests, the original Monocar was a single-seater, with a wheelbase of only 6 ft 6 in, and it was only 2 ft 6 in wide. It was not, in fairness, a very efficiently packaged car because, within three years, the famous Austin Seven appeared, used a shorter wheelbase, and could carry four people in tolerable comfort.

Although AV's workforce totalled 80 men, this light machine had spidery, minimal, bodywork by Thames Valley Pattern Works, made out of a combination of plywood, papier mâché and mahogany with some aluminium skin panels. Most of the cars seem to have been painted red, with black mudguards (or sometimes merely of polished aluminium). Steering was by wires which passed around strategically located bobbins (which could be very perilous, especially when the unlubricated bobbins began to wear, or fray). From the V-twin air-cooled JAP or Blackburne motorcycle engine, transmission was by chain, through a Sturmey Archer three-speed motorcycle gearbox.

Not even the very low price or weight (the first cars weighed only 600 lb, or twice that of a large motorcycle), could make the Monocar universally popular. Although this was a crude little machine, it was at least simple, and therefore easy to repair when things went wrong (as they often did). Later attempts to broaden its appeal by making it longer, with two tandem seats, or even as a wider Runabout with two parallel seats were not a success.

All cars of this type were eventually defeated by competition from the cheap Austin-Seven, and even from the bulkier Morris 'Bullnose' Cowley, and the last of several hundred AVs were built in 1924. AV reverted to selling other makes of car (notably Jowetts) and survived into the 1950s.

AV Monocar

Years in production: 1919–24
Structure: Rear-engine/rear-drive. Separate chassis
Engine type: Twin-cylinder, air-cooled, JAP or Blackburne
Bore and stroke: 70 x 85 mm, 76 x 85 mm or 85 x 85 mm
Capacity: 654, 770 or 864 cc
Power: Not quoted
Fuel supply: One Capac, or Claudel-Hobson, carburettor
Suspension: Beam-axle front, beam-axle rear
Weight: 600 lb
Top speed: 40 mph

Right: In the Monocar, the driving position was low, the occupant's legs being angled sharply forwards into the pointed nose, and to make this possible the engine was mounted in the tail, driving the rear wheels.

1920 Vauxhall 30/98

Vauxhall's early cars offered no great distinction, but that changed when L.H. Pomeroy was appointed as chief engineer. With a great love of high-performance engines and cars, he soon persuaded his new bosses that they should back a new sports car, and even dabble with Grand Prix racing. In 1910 the first hand-built sporting Vauxhalls appeared for use in the German Prince Henry trials. These were such a success that a series of road cars, the 'Prince Henry' models, went on sale at £600 each.

The first new Vauxhall model, the 30/98, was built in 1913, as a better, faster and more practical development of the Prince Henry, but its career, as a production car, really belongs to the years after the end of the First World War. With a larger engine than the Prince Henry, it was the fastest sports car of its day, guaranteed to reach 100 mph in stripped-out racing form. This, in effect, meant that it was the Jaguar E-type or McLaren F1 of its day, as it was so much quicker than any rival. The chassis price of £900, however, guaranteed that it would always be rare.

Vauxhall 30/98 (E-type)

Years in production: 1913–22
Structure: Front engine/rear-drive. Separate chassis
Engine type: 4-cylinder, side-valve
Bore and stroke: 98 x 150 mm
Capacity: 4,525 cc
Power: 90 bhp @ 3,000 rpm
Fuel supply: Single updraught Zenith carburettor
Suspension: Beam-axle front, beam-axle rear
Weight: 2,690 lb
Top speed: 85 mph

Production of this car, with a simple but effective side-valve engine, got under way properly in 1919, when it was known by the factory (and by the customers) as the 30/98 E-type model – this title following the use of B, C, and D-type Vauxhalls of the pre-war period. The original 30/98 was solidly built, which made it heavy, but it was also fast, and combined impressive performance with good roadholding by the standards of the 1920s. The snag was that its price – £1,670 at first, reduced to 'only' £1,300 in 1921 – made it a direct rival to the Bentley 3-litre, and both these cars were fighting for a very limited market.

About 270 cars were built before a redesign followed in 1922, which produced the equally-legendary OE-type. The main change was to the engine, which was converted to overhead-valve operation on advice from Ricardo (this explains the 'O' of the new title), and produced a rousing 115 bhp. It was an outstanding car, though increasingly this was measured by pre-war standards, and compared with the Bentley it was still a light motor car. Amazingly, the OE-type did not have four-wheel brakes (the Bentley always did), though towards the end of its run, from 1926, (at a chassis price of £950) a 120 bhp version was made available, with four-wheel brakes to control it all.

The last OE was produced in 1927 – two years after Vauxhall had been taken over by General Motors of the USA – there being 312 of that variant. Sadly, GM never again allowed Vauxhall to make such a distinguished machine.

Below: Solidly built with good roadholding for the 1920's, this car's price, £1,670, made it a direct rival to the Bentley 3-litre – both cars fought for a very limited market.

1921 Bentley 3-litre

W.O. Bentley made his name as an importer of French DFP sports cars before 1914, and for his BR air-cooled rotary aero-engined designs during it. In 1919 he decided to make a car of his own design.

The 3-litre, first seen at the 1919 Olympia Motor Show, was put into production at a factory near Staples Corner, on London's North Circular road, and was first sold in 1921: it was the first of a legendary pedigree of locomotive-like British sports cars. Indeed, it is true to say that the 4.5, 6.5 and 8-litre cars are all recognisably descended from the original 3-litre.

Chassis engineering was conventional in every way, but the engine aroused a great deal of interest. Massively built, tall and elegant, the four-cylinder unit was almost unique in having four valves per cylinder, and an overhead camshaft in a non-detachable cylinder head, a layout which gave the

Bentley 3-litre

Years in production: 1921–28
Structure: Front engine/rear-drive. Separate chassis
Engine type: 4-cylinder, single overhead camshaft
Bore and stroke: 80 x 149 mm
Capacity: 2,996 cc
Power: 80 bhp @ unspecified rpm
Fuel supply: One Smith/two horizontal SU carburettors
Suspension: Beam-axle front, beam-axle rear
Weight: 2,800 lb
Top speed: 80 mph

Bentley 3-litre a sparkling performance.

Even though Bentley always seemed to be under-capitalised (it came close to bankruptcy at least three times in the 1920s, before the final collapse in 1931) W.O. Bentley himself always found the time and the money to enter his cars in an ambitious programme of races and high-speed record attempts, telling everyone that this would not only improve development, but would also bring valuable publicity. It was the Le Mans 24 Hours race which meant most to Bentley, where lightweight and tuned-up 3-litres won the race in 1923 and 1927. His cars also raced with distinction in the British Tourist Trophy race (second in 1922), and even in the Indianapolis 500, where W.D. Hawkes's car averaged 81 mph.

The Speed Model, with a tuned-up engine, arrived in 1924, and following the development of the 4.5-litre model (this engine being a technical amalgam of the 3-litre and 6.5-litre 'six' units) a number of common parts were specified. There were three distinct sets of gearbox ratios. The original chassis price was £1,100, which was usually raised to about £1,400, depending on the type of bodywork chosen. By any standards this made the Bentley an extremely expensive proposition, so to stimulate sales the 'Standard' chassis price dropped to £895 in 1924.

Below: Bentley was so confident of his engineering skills that a five-year warranty was offered for the chassis assembly. Three-litre types were in production for seven years, in several basic forms and in three wheelbase lengths.

1923 Sunbeam 12

To many vintage car enthusiasts, there has only ever been one real Sunbeam company – that which built cars in Wolverhampton before 1936. Sunbeam, thereafter, became an unwilling part of the Rootes Group, and it was not long before new Sunbeam models had lost their pedigree, and were really no more than Hillmans or Humbers in party dress.

The original Sunbeams of 1901 were weird little creations with wheels in a diamond, rather than conventional formation (and with imported De Dion engines), but Sunbeam's great independent years began in 1909 after the celebrated designer Louis Coatalen joined the company. A range of newly-engineered four-cylinder and six-cylinder types emerged, the 12/16 being such an outstanding car that series production was taken over by Rover during the First World War, to maintain supply for the armed forces.

Sunbeam amalgamated with Talbot and Darracq in 1920 to form the STD combine, and though Coatalen always preferred to design sports, even racing, cars, most touring Sunbeams of the period were cars of great refinement but not outstanding performance. The new generation 12-30 of 1923 was altogether more representative of the genre. Here was a car so typical of the middle class British touring car of the period that the vintage 'rules of engagement' might have been written around it. Both this, and the much larger 16-50 were an evolution of the popular 14 chassis (whose roots lay in a Darracq design), which had been in production for some time, though with new engines, and updated body styles.

The chassis was simple but robust, with channel-section side members, and pressed cross-bracing members, front and rear suspension was by leaf springs (the rear axle being suspended on full cantilever springs), and the 10-spoke wheels were of what was still known as the 'artillery' type. Low-slung by 1920s standards, the frame actually sat well up above the line of the two axles, with the driver sitting atop the frame, not inside the side members. It was still acceptable to fit brakes solely to the rear wheels of this 1.5-litre car, although front brakes became more common as the 1920s progressed.

The engine was a simple, low-revving, rugged overhead-valve four-cylinder unit. It was 1,598 cc instead of the 2,121 cc of the 14 hp model, and was backed by a three-speed transmission, and a gear lever positioned to the outside of the driver's seat.

As with other vintage cars of the period, two immediate problems faced the 12-30, one being that it was obviously based on a larger type, the other being that it was expensive at £570. Although it was better built, with more individual components than the Bullnose Morris, it was no faster, nor did it have better roadholding. Only about 95 cars were ever built.

Sunbeam 12

Years in production: 1923–26
Structure: Front engine/rear-drive. Separate chassis
Engine type: 4-cylinder, overhead-valve
Bore and stroke: 68 x 110 mm
Capacity: 1,598 cc
Power: 12 bhp
Fuel supply: Single Claudel-Hobson carburettor
Suspension: Beam-axle front, beam-axle rear

Right: Typical of the British touring car of the period, the Sunbeam 12 was an expensive car but its roadholding and speed were no better than those of the 'Bullnose' Morris.

1923 Trojan

The best way to describe the Trojan is as eccentric, for its design flew in the face of almost every trend and accepted practice of the period. Leslie Hounsfield laid out this mid-engined machine so well and so successfully, however, that Leyland (the truck specialists), adopted the design and put it into production at Ham, near Kingston-upon-Thames in 1922.

No performance car, and certainly not a looker, it nevertheless appealed to so many that more than 16,000 cars were built in the 1920s alone. Although a Trojan Utility looked conventional enough apart from the radiator and the fuel tank, there was almost nothing under the bonnet, for the hilariously simple (and in theory, quite impractical) two-stroke engine was situated under the rear floor, driving the rear wheels through a two-speed and reverse epicyclic gearbox. The 'self-starter' was a ratchetted lever on the floor, to the right of the driver.

The chassis was a rigid punt-type platform, and although there was plenty of ground clearance and soft cantilever leaf springs at front and rear, the ride was not helped by the presence of very thin, solid tyres. All this, the slow and utterly metronomic quality of the long-stroke engine, and the ability to change gear without a clutch pedal (although one was provided to make timid drivers feel at home), made the Trojan an acquired taste.

The fact that it was an extremely simple vintage car, costing little to run, and almost nothing to maintain (many reached 100,000 miles needing little more than a periodic de-coking of the engine), meant that it soon established its own market, though motoring pundits were never impressed. One of the Trojan's greatest fans, historian Anthony Bird, pointed out that it was almost comic in everything it did, that many professional testers 'praised it with faint damns', and that the motor trade itself was openly hostile to a machine which rarely gave them any work.

No-one bought a Trojan if they were in a hurry, for at any speed above 25 mph, the hammering transmitted through the solid tyres from the poor roads of the period could be extremely uncomfortable. On the other hand, because of its good low-speed engine torque, and its solid rear axle (no differential was fitted), it was a car for climbing every hill, even in the most appalling weather.

One very important, high-profile, fleet contract was obtained: from Brooke Bond, the tea manufacturers, who bought more than 5,000 Trojans over the years for delivery van use, and kept them almost indefinitely, so in cities, at least, the Trojan was always prominent.

Assembly by Leyland ended in 1926, but was revived by Hounsfield himself a year later, in Croydon. Updated only as necessary (which was very little), the 'Utility' became the 'Ten', and maintained a following until the mid-1930s, when car production finally ended.

Trojan

Years in production: 1922–29
Structure: Mid-engine/rear-drive. Separate chassis
Engine type: 4-cylinder, two-stroke
Bore and stroke: 63.5 x 117.5 mm
Capacity: 1,488 cc
Power: 11 bhp @ 1,200 rpm
Fuel supply: One Trojan or Amal carburettor
Suspension: Beam-axle front, beam-axle rear
Weight: 1,315 lb
Top speed: 32 mph

Above: Although this car had a large bonnet behind the radiator, the engine was positioned under the rear floor. The solid tyres made any journey very uncomfortable on the poor road surfaces of the time.

1923 Austin Seven

For years, in the 1920s and 1930s, the tiny Austin Seven was a best-selling little car, which set every standard of small packaging; it seemed cheeky, simple, and promised low-cost motoring. In many ways, it was similar to the Mini which followed decades later.

Everything about the car – everything, including the engine transmission, suspension and choice of bodies – was brand new, for here was a car designed to weigh no more than 800 lb/363 kg, and to be the first (and lowest-priced) car which any new motorist would consider. Initially on sale at £165, (in the UK, only the mass-produced Ford Model T was cheaper), it provided unbeatable value, for although a Seven was slow (anyone who drove faster than about 35 mph was a masochist), and had precarious handling and brakes, it had enormous appeal. The fact that it was worth only pennies by the time it was five years old didn't seem to matter, for even old and rusty Sevens would keep motoring.

The A-profiled (in plan) chassis frame was flimsy and flexible, with a transverse leaf spring at the front, and with cantilever leaf spring at the rear, the brakes rather a bad joke, and the 'in-and-out' clutch fierce in the extreme. It was almost impossible to provide comfortable four-seater bodywork inside the 75 in/1900 mm wheelbase, but Austin tried hard, and sold tens of thousands of these angular machines every year. At first the tiny 747 cc engine produced a mere 10.5 bhp, but this increased gradually over the years, culminating at 17 bhp in the mid-1930s; by this time an Austin Seven could reach more than 50 mph.

Although it was already looking obsolete by the early 1930s, regular re-touching, not only to the style but also to the engineering, meant that it was invariably Austin's best-selling model, and before the last car was produced in 1939, more than 290,000 of all types had been sold. At its peak, which lasted for more than a decade, well over 20,000 cars were being sold, every year. In later life the engine found further use in Reliant three wheelers, and a passion for racing, encouraged by the 750 MC, saw power outputs pushed up to extraordinary levels.

Right: Most factory-built Sevens were two-door saloons or tourers, with a very square style (one could almost say non-style), but there were many special coachwork styles, and even the occasional two-seater.

Austin Seven

Years in production: 1923–39
Structure: Front engine/rear-drive. Separate chassis
Engine type: 4-cylinder, side-valve
Bore and stroke: 56 x 76.2 mm
Capacity: 747 cc
Power: 10.5 bhp @ 2,400 rpm
Fuel supply: One updraught Zenith carburettor
Suspension: Beam-axle front, beam-axle rear
Weight: 800 lb
Top speed: 40 mph

1924 Bean 12

Although glamorous cars like the massive Bentleys, and sports cars such as the Frazer Nash made most of the headlines at the time, the 'vintage era' – roughly speaking the 1920s – saw many more worthy, rather individual, and charming (though slow) family cars go on sale. The Bean, from Dudley, in the West Midlands, was a very popular example of that type.

Bean shot to fame and back to obscurity in only ten years during the 1920s. The business was established immediately after the First World War (the original Bean was actually a remodelling of the 'Perry' light car) and produced more than 4,000 cars a year in the middle of the period. It rapidly faded as the 'Hatfield Bean' and failed to survive the marketing onslaught from cheaper cars like the Morris Cowley and Oxford.

The first Bean of 1919 was a stolidly-engineered and styled 12 hp model (or '11.9'). The factory at Tipton, Dudley was well-capitalised, but the company's ambitions stretched their finances, and survival was always a struggle.

The Bean 12 was updated in 1924, and the larger, heavier and longer 14 was produced in the same year. Rugged but unexciting, both types had a four-cylinder side-valve engine (the 14 having a 2,386 cc type); the 12 had a separate three-speed, while the 14's engine was in a unit with a four-speed gearbox. In both cases the performance was no more than adequate by the standards of the day. Many customers, however, did not mind this, especially as the national speed limit was a mere 20 mph.

Beans were relatively modern and well specified for 1925. Prices ranged from £335 to £395 for the 12 hp, and from £375 for a three-seater Tourer 14, to £585 for a well equipped saloon.

The mid-1920s, however, were the high point for Bean, which had once talked of selling 10,000 cars every year, but never came close to achieving that mark. Although cheaper (and better) than many of their rivals, they were coming under increasing competition from Austin and Morris, with the cheapest Morris Cowley retailing for no more than £175.

By developing a Meadows six-cylinder engined car (the 18/50), Bean found itself saddled with more capital expenditure than it could handle in the long term; other expensive models did not sell as well as planned, and the last cars (but not commercial vehicles) were made in 1929. No fewer than 10,000 11.9s and 4,000 14s were built, figures which dwarfed those achieved by the later models.

Right: From end to end, this was a typical vintage family car, with a high, sturdy chassis, a low revving side-valve engine, and artillery-pattern road wheels with four-wheel brakes and shock absorbers all round.

Bean 12

Years in production: 1919–27
Structure: Front engine/rear-drive. Separate chassis
Engine type: 4-cylinder, side-valve
Bore and stroke: 69 x 120 mm
Capacity: 1,795 cc
Power: Not stated
Fuel supply: Single Zenith carburettor
Suspension: Beam-axle front, beam-axle rear
Weight: 1,550 lb
Top speed: 45 mph

1925 Frazer Nash 'Chain-gang'

No car as special and as uniquely-conceived, as the 'Chain-gang' Frazer Nash comes into existence without precedent. In this case, designer, Archie Frazer Nash, had already been involved in the GN business, where he had proved the worth of the extremely simple, but effective, chain drive transmission.

Setting up on his own in Kingston-on-Thames (though assembly soon moved to Isleworth, in Middlesex), Frazer Nash decided to make a sports car so simply engineered that it could be dismantled like a gigantic Meccano set (some owners got very used to doing this!), which would use proprietary water-cooled four-cylinder or six-cylinder engines, and a four-speed-and-reverse transmission with dog engagement of various sprockets linked by chain to the rear axle. The first were delivered in 1924, the last in 1939, by which time their popularity had ended.

Chassis were very simple, with stiff cantilever leaf springs at front and rear (Archie Frazer Nash was said to have been mortally offended if any one of

Frazer Nash 'Chain-gang'

Years in production: 1924–39
Structure: Front engine/rear-drive. Separate chassis
TYPICAL, WITH MEADOWS ENGINE:
Engine type: 4-cylinder, overhead-valve
Bore and stroke: 69 x 100 mm
Capacity: 1,496 cc
Power: 62 bhp @ 4,500 rpm
Fuel supply: Two horizontal SU carburettors
Suspension: Beam-axle front, beam-axle rear
Weight: 1,800 lb
Top speed: 85 mph

these was seen to deflect) and high-geared steering. Highly responsive handling was therefore assured.

The chain drive layout was so simple that critics often questioned its efficiency: the drawbacks were that chains could, and often did, snap, and the links had to be cleaned and oiled at least every 500 miles. There was no torque-splitting differential, so the Nash needed a narrow rear track to ensure that tyres were not prematurely worn out: traction, on the other hand, was excellent.

Because the 'Chain gang' (the reason for the nick-name is quite obvious) was light and handled so well, its competitive potential was obvious, even though the styling (and the poor aerodynamic shape) never allowed high speeds to be attained. Over the years, more suitable engines were chosen. Original cars had Power Plus units; British Anzani followed, and Meadows overhead-valve types powered the first batch of 'TT Replica' examples. There was even the choice of twin-cam Blackburne six-cylinder units, and a single-cam 'Gough four'. Many variants were named after sporting successes: 'Shelsley' after the British hillclimb, 'Boulogne' after a French racing circuit, and of course 'TT Replica' after the Tourist Trophy race in the Isle of Man where the cars performed so well.

Below: Low, narrow, open to the elements, and utterly single-purpose, these were singular cars for the individualist. Only about 350 were built in 15 years.

1925 Rolls-Royce Phantom I

'How do you improve on perfection?' was one remark made by Rolls-Royce devotees when the New Phantom eventually succeeded the long-running 40/50 hp Silver Ghost in 1925. But this was to ignore the obvious, which was that the older car had gradually fallen behind the times, mechanically at least, and was overdue for replacement.

To replace one icon with another, Rolls-Royce decided to tackle the job in two stages, first by providing a new overhead-valve six-cylinder engine, and other chassis innovation such as four-wheel brakes; second, an entirely new chassis was developed, which would appear later, and form the basis of the Phantom II. As the new car would have the same bulk as before, and as all Rolls-Royce styling was provided by outside coachbuilders, many potential customers might not even notice the transition.

For the new car, Rolls-Royce produced its second overhead-valve engine (the first had appeared in the new 'small' Rolls-Royce, the 20 hp, in 1922. This was smoother, more modern, and more powerful than before, but otherwise set out to do the same unobtrusive job. Then, as ever, Rolls-Royce motoring was not about performance, but about dignity, silence, almost infallible reliability, and the ability to insulate its owners almost entirely from their surroundings.

The new chassis, therefore, slipped quietly into production, while principal comment seemed to be about styles (the famous radiator grille was not modified), and the details of equipment and furnishing. Rolls-Royce took the big step of producing New Phantoms at a factory in the USA, at Springfield, Massachusetts, where bodies were provided by North American coachbuilders, and were often more flamboyant than their European equivalents.

Purchasers of New Phantoms rarely worried about roadholding, performance and fuel consumption, but if their cars were less than dependable or silent, complaints would surely follow. For some large cars, in any case, this was still the era of the chauffeur, so for the owner (or the occupant, for were bought by companies) it was more important that a New Phantom should have a magnificently trimmed rear compartment with plenty of fittings with which to impress one's colleagues.

And so it did, for no fewer than 2,212 new Phantoms were built at Derby in just four years, with another 1,241 being produced in the USA until American production ended in 1931.

Below: The successor to the Silver Ghost, the Phantom had a new overhead six-cylinder engine, a new chassis and four-wheel brakes. The new engine was smoother and more powerful than before.

Rolls-Royce Phantom I

Years in production: 1925–29
Structure: Front engine/rear-drive. Separate chassis
Engine type: 6-cylinder, overhead-valve
Bore and stroke: 104 x 139.7 mm
Capacity: 7,668 cc
Power: Never revealed
Fuel supply: Single Rolls-Royce carburettor
Suspension: Beam-axle front, beam-axle rear
Weight: Up to 6,500 lb (dependent on body fitted)
Top speed: 80–85 mph (dependent on body fitted)

1926 MG 14/28

Cecil Kimber, General Manager of Morris Garages, in Oxford started by building special-bodied Morris Bullnose cars in 1923, and made them even more distinguished by adopting the MG (or Morris Garages) badge. The original MG-badged cars were not as sporting as those which followed, but they established a famous sports car marque.

Like the first Morris 'specials' which had preceded them in 1923, the MG 14/28 types were based on the simple chassis and running gear of the mass-produced Morris Bullnose, but now they had larger and more powerful engines, and even more distinctive body styling. During the life of the car, engines became more distinctive, for all were stripped, rebuilt and modified by the Morris Garages' mechanics. At first the cars were assembled in a corner of the Morris workshops at Alfred's Lane, Oxford, the chassis being delivered direct from Morris's Cowley factory on the outskirts of the city. Kimber's craftsmen then made a multitude of improvements, including flattening the springs, re-raking the steering, changing the suspension dampers and altering the overall gearing.

Early MGs used the well known Bullnose radiator, but with the MG octagon badge fixed to it, though from late 1926 these were replaced by a more MG-like flat-nose style. Coachbuilding skills were prolific the time, and it was easy for Kimber to find bodies in two-seat, four-seat and a variety of saloon styles and shapes; Carbodies of Coventry provided most of them.

To call this pioneering MG a 'super sports' was really advertiser's hype (at which Kimber was adept), but there was no lack of demand for the model. The first two-seaters cost £350, though one could pay up to £460 for a four-seater saloon. The first factory move (to Bainton Road) followed in 1925, and further expansion would follow in 1927.

These sporty and extrovert machines were further improved in 1927 with the introduction of the revised Morris 'flat-nose' chassis, which was shorter, stiffer and heavier. Before long, production had risen above ten cars a week, but this was only the first of many expansions. The restless Kimber was not content to leave the 14/28 unmodified for long, so it was joined by a very similar car called the 14/40 in 1927, though the changes were mainly cosmetic. By 1928, however, MG had more exciting models under development – including the first of the tiny Midgets – so this pioneering MG model was soon phased out. Although about 1,300 14/28s and 14/40s of all types were built, very few now survive.

MG 14/28

Years in production: 1924–29
Structure: Front engine/rear-drive. Separate chassis
Engine type: 4-cylinder, side-valve
Bore and stroke: 75 x 102 mm
Capacity: 1,802 cc
Power: 35 bhp @ 4,000 rpm
Fuel supply: One horizontal Solex or SU carburettor
Suspension: Beam-axle front, beam-axle rear
Weight: 2,210 lb
Top speed: 65 mph

Below: Although the engines were modified from mundane side-valve Morris 'Oxford' types, they pushed out a creditable 30–35 bhp, which was enough to give the cars a 60–65 mph top speed.

1927 Riley Brooklands

Once Riley had announced its brand-new, and technically advanced twin-high camshaft 1,087 cc engine, complete with part-spherical combustion chambers, it became a prime target for sporting use. Even though Riley had not, so far, made a small sports car, the temptation to break into this new market was immense. The result, first seen in 1927, was the wickedly low and purposeful 'Brooklands' two-seater.

The engine had already been used in the Riley Nine family car of 1926, which was selling well, and clearly had a great deal of potential. Race driver and entrepreneur J.G. Parry Thomas had already started work on a 'Brooklands Special' before he was killed in a Land Speed Record attempt, and his work was continued by Reid Railton.

The first, and so far only, car was shown in mid 1927, with a unique low short-wheelbase chassis frame, and skimpy two-seater bodywork. A production version, the 'Speed Model', was put on sale months later, though this car had another totally different type of frame, a two-piece full-width screen and some rather skimpy all-weather equipment to make it more practical for road use. Priced at £395, and with a 50 bhp version of the engine (which was a very high specific output by late 1920s standards), it was obviously a fast little machine.

Riley Brooklands

Years in production: 1927–32
Structure: Front engine/rear-drive. Separate chassis
Engine type: 4-cylinder, over head-valve
Bore and stroke: 60.3 x 95.2 mm
Capacity: 1,087 cc
Power: 50 bhp @ 5,000 rpm
Fuel supply: Two horizontal SU (or Solex) carburettors
Suspension: Beam-axle front, beam-axle rear
Weight: Never specified
Top speed: 80 mph

The whole car was tiny, light, nervous in its handling, and had a top speed of more than 80 mph (which made cars like the original MG M-type Midget look very slow indeed), though there was obviously much more to come as Reid Railton's race car lapped Brooklands at 98.62 mph on its very first outing. Almost immediately in 1929 it became known as the 'Brooklands' Riley, a glamorous nickname for any machine, particularly one priced at £420. With the aid of sponsored runs in long-distance trials like the Land's End (where Sammy Davis's car won a Gold Medal), it was soon seen to be versatile, strong, and very likeable.

No-one ever bought a Brooklands as a runabout, no-one attempted to carry more than two friendly occupants, and there was never any question of transporting luggage or even many parts. It was, after all, a hard-sprung, super-sporting, utterly convincing sports car (or perhaps a competition sports car?), which made no compromises, and it was well loved because of that. The market for this car was very limited, however, and although Riley are known to have produced at least 30,000 Nines of all types, only 200 of them were Brooklands models.

Below and right: In its day, the Brooklands was an immensely appealing little car, with low lines, purposeful detailing, and not a line, or superfluous bit of kit, out of place.

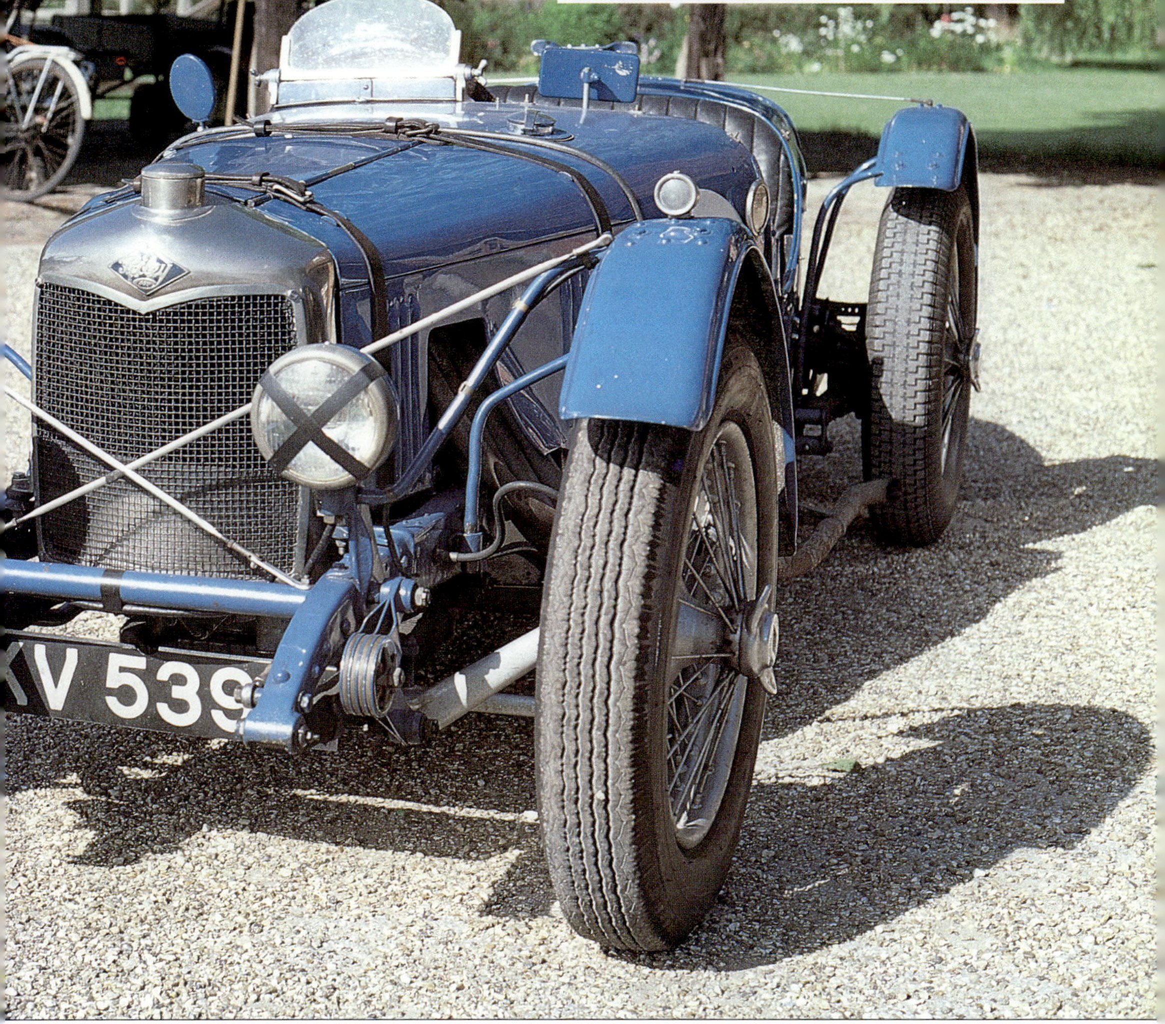

1928 Invicta 4½-litre

The Invicta was a short-lived and essentially 'vintage' phenomenon, but its reputation lives on. Conceived by Noel Macklin, and financed by the Lyle family (the sugar millionaires) in the 1920s, a range of fine hand-built machines emerged from Surrey and were only on the market from 1925 to 1933. Smaller Invictas followed, but Macklin had already turned his enthusiasm to making American-based Railtons instead, and post-war Invictas died through lack of custom.

Each and every 'vintage' Invicta was a sporting car; most were open, and all had that indefinable 'built like a battleship' quality which Bentley had already made so familiar to British motorists. The company was small, and under-equipped, so Invicta only changed their design slowly, and used a large number of 'bought-in' or proprietary components, particularly their engines. Original Invictas used a Coventry-Climax engine, but from 1925 the team turned to Henry Meadows of Wolverhampton, who supplied its rugged six-cylinder power unit in a variety of sizes, most notably the famous 4½-litre size, which was also supplied to Lagonda and other concerns.

Apart from the impressive front-end styling, which featured riveted bonnet panels, and in imitation of the contemporary Rolls-Royce, the cars' styling was unexceptional.

By 1930 the 4½-litre Invicta was available in two forms: as the high-chassis 'A' type, and the entirely different and much-lowered 'S' type, both at prices which approached those of the current Bentley and Rolls-Royce vehicles. The S-type (sometimes nicknamed the 'flat iron') Invicta was usually supplied with a lightweight open sports car body, and could be an extremely successful competition car.

Although one car (driven by *The Autocar*'s sports editor, Sammy Davis) was involved in a lurid crash at Brooklands, another in the hands of Donald Healey won the 1931 Monte Carlo Rally. Built like a battleship, and with the sort of stump-pulling torque for which such vintage engines were famous, this was a car which appealed strongly to those who could afford one. Yet by the early 1930s, rich sportsmen were few and increasingly cautious with their money, so Invicta found itself running out of clients. According to Noel Macklin, there were two solutions: one was to produce a much smaller-engined car (which was a complete failure); the other was to turn to an altogether cheaper type of car, which appeared as the Railton.

All in all, no more than 500 4½-litre Invictas were ever made, only 77 being the charismatic S-type sports cars.

Below: Every one of the original Invictas was developed around the same general chassis layout, which featured rock-hard half-elliptical front and rear suspension, and rod-operated drum brakes which were often inadequate for the car's performance.

Invicta 4½ litre

Years in production: 1928–33
Structure: Front engine/rear-drive. Separate chassis
Engine type: 6-cylinder, overhead-valve
Bore and stroke: 88.5 x 120.6 mm
Capacity: 4,467 cc
Power: 115 bhp @ unspecified rpm
Fuel supply: Two horizontal SU carburettors
Suspension: Beam-axle front, beam-axle rear
Weight: 2,800 lb
Top speed: 90–95 mph

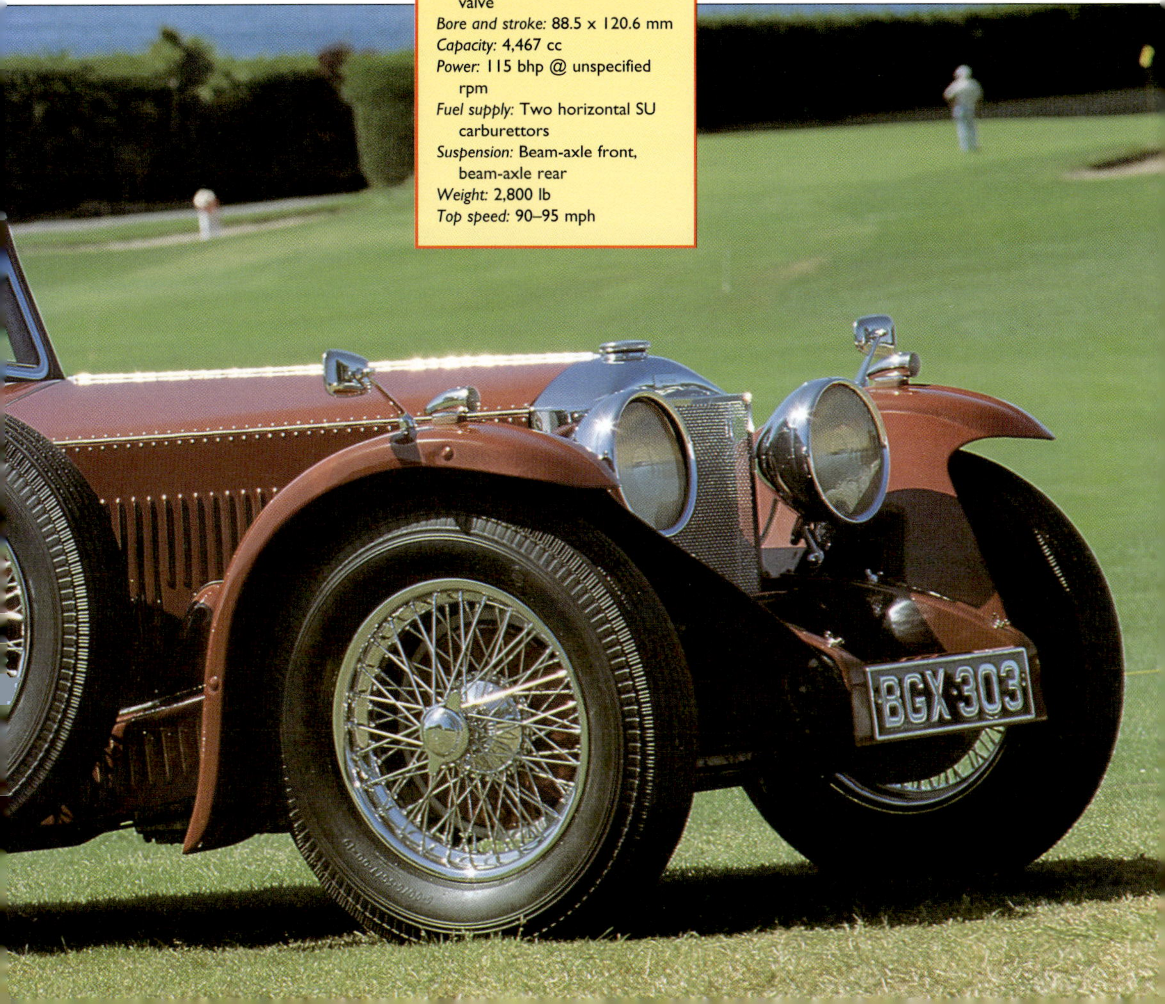

1929 BSA 3-wheeler

BSA of Birmingham was famous for many years as a manufacturer of guns and other armaments, before it started to make cars. The fact that it was already producing motor cycles, and had acquired Daimler in 1910, must have influenced its plan to produce small, cheap, cars, as a half-way house between the two types.

Although the original BSA car of 1921–25 was a four-wheeler with an air-cooled power unit, the second model which followed in 1929, was a quirky and individualistic three-wheeler. With two front wheels and a single rear, but with front-wheel-drive (itself a real novelty) this was a distinctive and surprisingly successful car for the next few years. In seven years, until further rationalisation of the business ensued, BSA built at least 5,200 machines at its motorcycle factory at Small Heath, Birmingham.

Only a company as well founded as BSA could have produced a car like this, particularly as it reached maturity in the depths of Britain's depression. Although Morgan had already linked air-cooled two-cylinder engines to three-wheeler motoring, this was the first British application of front-wheel-drive; on the BSA, the rear wheel's only use was to hold the rear end of the 'duck-tail' bodywork off the ground.

The air-cooled 90-degree V-twin engine had overhead valves, and was a Hotchkiss design, a modified version of that used in the earlier BSA Ten of the early 1920s. Unlike any other engine of its day, it drove forward to a three-speed gearbox, which powered the front wheels, independent front suspension being by clusters of cantilever quarter-elliptic leaf springs.

Although this was no sports car (the engine, whose power was not stated, was not nearly as powerful as that of the Morgan three-wheeler) it was a brisk and surprisingly willing runabout, usually sold as a rather flimsily built two-seater (or three-abreast, if everyone was friendly) soft-top. Cruising speeds were no higher than 40 mph, but with complete car prices starting at no more than £130, it was an intriguing alternative to contemporary four-wheelers like the Austin Seven and the Morris Minor.

BSA persevered with this car for several years, making a few four-wheeler models (FW32 types) in 1932, while a four-cylinder water-cooled engine type followed in 1933.

Below: The chassis frame was simplicity itself, with members surrounding the engine/transmission unit, and with a single backbone member leading back to a neat cantilever spring/trailing link type of rear wheel suspension.

BSA 3-wheeler

Years in production: 1929–36
Structure: Front engine/front-wheel-drive. Separate chassis
Engine type: V2-cylinder, side-valve
Bore and stroke: 85 x 90 mm
Capacity: 1,021 cc
Power: Not revealed
Fuel supply: Single updraught Solex carburettor
Suspension: Independent front, independent rear
Weight: Never specified
Top speed: 50 mph

1929 Daimler Double Six

Between 1908 and the mid 1930s, Daimler of Coventry built a string of famous sleeve-valve-engined cars, with smooth and unobtrusive power units, which produced a slight but characteristic blue haze of engine oil smoke. The most famous of all, and a genuinely successful rival to Rolls-Royce, was the Double Six family, first launched in 1926.

Daimler's chief engineer, Laurence Pomeroy (Senior) persuaded his directors to authorise a series of magnificent and complicated V12 engines, which used many existing parts from current Daimler six-cylinder power units. It was called 'Double Six' because in many ways, such as the duplication of carburation, water pump and ignition systems, it was a double six-cylinder unit. The original, massive and imperial 'Fifty' was effectively two sets of 25/85 six-cylinder blocks set at an angle of 60 degrees.

With a capacity of 7.1 litres, and a declared output of 150 bhp (Rolls-Royce never dared to reveal their own peak figures, which were not impressive), this provided a huge, silent, power unit with more torque, which was ideal for the powering of massive limousines and (occasional) fast sporting models. Lever-type hydraulic dampers were standardised, and a vacuum servo was definitely needed to help power up the four-wheel drum brakes. Naturally, there was no power-assistance for the steering (such systems had not yet been invented), so the chauffeur had a hard job. Later models, at least, were available with Daimler's new pre-selector/fluid-flywheel transmission, which made them even smoother than before.

The typical Double Six '50' had a lofty limousine body, which could seat up to seven people, might weigh 6,200 lb/2,812 kg, and would cost around £2,500 – definitely Rolls-Royce levels. Not surprisingly, this model was popular with the British royal family, who purchased several, over the years. Fuel consumption could be worse than 10 mpg, but no-one seemed to worry about that.

To expand the range in 1928, the '50' was joined by the Double Six '30', which had an altogether different and smaller 3.8-litre V12; this model itself was replaced by the 5.3-litre '30/40' in 1930.

Even without the effects of the Depression, Double Six sales would always have been low, but economic problems hurt their prospects further, so the programme was gradually run down during the early 1930s, and the cars were eventually replaced with conventional straight-eight cylinder/poppet-valve cars. Less than 500 Double Six cars were built in the 1920s, even fewer after that.

Below: Chassis, though conventional in design, were always colossal, typically with a wheel-base of 155.5 in/3950 mm or even 163 in/4140 mm.

Daimler Double Six

Years in production: 1927–30 (1931–35 as developed 40/50 model)
Structure: Front engine/rear-drive Separate chassis
Engine type: V12-cylinder, double sleeve-valve
Bore and stroke: 81.5 x 114 mm
Capacity: 7,136 cc
Power: 150 bhp @ 2,480 rpm
Fuel supply: Two updraught Daimler carburettors (one per bank)
Suspension: Beam-axle front, beam-axle rear
Weight: Up to 6,200 lb (dependent on body fitted)
Top speed: 80 mph (dependent on body fitted)

1929 Talbot 14/45

Although the British Talbot concern was part of the larger Anglo-French Sunbeam-Talbot-Darracq (STD) combine, it was struggling to stay in business when Swiss-born engineer Georges Roesch returned to the company in London in 1925. Starting with a new six-cylinder engine, in the 14/45 of 1926, he transformed the prospects of the business, and was only ousted when Talbot fell into the hands of the Rootes Group in 1935.

Faced with almost non-existent sales of the older models, which had ageing technical features, Roesch was encouraged to start again – and did, from the ground up. The first of the new-generation cars was the 14/45. Its chassis, like that of the other 'Roesch Talbots' which would follow, was conventional enough, but the engine was quite superb.

Even in original form, when it measured a mere 1,666 cc, and had only four crankshaft main bearings, it seemed to be years ahead of contemporary British opposition: in later years, developed, enlarged and even more magnificent, it

Talbot 14/45

Years in production: 1926–35
Structure: Front engine/rear-drive. Separate chassis
Engine type: 4-cylinder, overhead-valve
Bore and stroke: 61 x 95 mm
Capacity: 1,666 cc
Power: 46 bhp @ 4,500 rpm
Fuel supply: One Zenith carburettor
Suspension: Beam-axle front, beam-axle rear
Weight: 2,630 lb
Top speed: 65 mph

would reach 3,377 cc and 123 bhp. At first it had only a single carburettor, but its potential was obvious.

The 14/45 model started life as a full five-seater saloon on a 120 in/3048 mm wheelbase. Other bodies – open, closed, 'family' and sporting – soon followed, and renamed the '65', the car sold until 1935. Clearly under-powered (or too heavy, depending on one's viewpoint), it was a car at the very beginning of its development life, but the quality of its engineering shone out from every corner. The asking price of £485 in 1926 ensured that it was a hit, and order books were immediately full, to the very limit of the North Kensington factory's capacity. Soon at least 50 14/45s were being built every week.

The chassis itself was neatly detailed, with deep side members and sturdy cross-bracing, and came complete with quarter-elliptic leaf spring rear suspension, a right-hand gear change, and torque tube transmission to the spiral bevel rear axle. Bodies were neat and impressive, rather than beautiful, but it was the obvious potential of the design, particularly of the engine, which attracted so much custom.

Motor traders, they say, did not like the new-fangled 14/45s because they required skilled, specialist attention, but the customers loved them. The handling was good, the quality of the engineering was high, and future prospects were enormous. By 1930 Roesch had developed the Talbot 90, with its 2.3-litre engine, the 3.0-litre-engined Talbot 105 followed in 1931, and an impressive string of race and rally results ensued. It was no wonder that the 14/45 was so popular, and before it finally died out (as the 65) no fewer than 11,851 cars had been produced.

Left: With good handling and high quality of engineering on these cars, customers flocked to buy this impressive five-seater saloon.

1931 Standard Big Nine

Until the end of the 1920s, Standard was a relatively small Coventry car maker, but the advent of Captain John Black, first as general manager, and later as managing director, galvanised it into further expansion. Black wanted Standard to be one of the 'big six' manufacturers, an ambition he achieved partly thanks to popular mass-market cars like the 'Big Nine'.

Like the Ford Model T (which had already disappeared) and the Ford 8 Model Y which soon followed, the Big Nine was intended to serve the mass market at a price they could afford, so it was engineered and equipped accordingly. Supported by Standard's ever-growing dealer chain, it was the sort of car the emerging middle class motorist could buy, use for business or enjoy at weekends: commuting, as a habit, was still rare in those days.

Standard Big Nine

Years in production: 1930–33
Structure: Front engine/rear-drive. Separate chassis
Engine type: 4-cylinder, side-valve
Bore and stroke: 63.5 x 102 mm
Capacity: 1,287 cc
Power: 25 bhp @ 3,200 rpm
Fuel supply: One Zenith carburettor
Suspension: Beam-axle front, beam-axle rear
Weight: 1,960 lb
Top speed: 54 mph

The first of the Big Nines was launched in 1928, and was one of the first Standards to use a new type of four-cylinder side-valve engine which (in four-cylinder and six-cylinder form) would find a home in many Standards and SS models in the next decade. The definitive Big Nine of 1930, though, was the first to combine coil ignition, a spiral bevel axle, and a new radiator style – but, unlike its predecessors, no union flag badge or mascot.

In many ways the first of Standard's mass-production cars, it influenced the Standards of the early 1930s in many ways, with its angular six-light saloon body style, its simple engine and transmissions (a choice of three-speed or four-speed), and its amazingly low prices, which started at only £195. In spite of what the traditionalists would insist, many aspiring motorists had not been able to afford a hand-built 'vintage' car, and it was this type of mass-produced machinery which was eventually going to put them on the road.

This was not a quick car, for its comfortable, and natural, cruising speed was no more than 40-45 mph, but at least it could record up to 40 mpg in daily use, and was simple, robust, and easy to service and maintain. In its road test, *The Autocar* called it 'a remarkably attractive car, especially in view of its moderate price.' Tens of thousands of Big Nines were eventually made, and their characteristics passed to the later, more stylish, Flying Nines; Standard's future was assured.

Below: The Standard Big Nine was a car intended to serve the mass market at a price they could afford and was easy to service and maintain.

1932 Alvis Speed Twenty

Although the first Alvis cars were not sold until 1920, they rapidly built up a fine reputation in the vintage era, not only because they were solidly-constructed machines, but because they had a great deal of sporting character too. While T.G. John was managing director, and Capt. G.T. Smith-Clarke was chief design engineer, the marque's future was safe.

During the 1920s a series of cars had all used the same type of four-cylinder engine, but the first six-cylinder Alvis, the 1,870 cc 14.75 SA, appeared in 1927. It was this engine and its enlarged descendants which powered almost every subsequent Alvis made until the outbreak of war in 1939. The original engine was later bored out, given a longer stroke, and generally modernised as the years passed, for it was an ideal 'building block' for Alvis's future. From 1,870 cc, it became 2,148 cc, then 2,511 cc, 2,762 cc – and there was still more to come.

The Speed Twenty (the title indicated its official British RAC rating) was launched in 1931 as one of Alvis's first true post-vintage thoroughbred models, and came complete with the ex-Silver Eagle power unit of 2,511 cc. For the time, its peak power rating – 87 bhp – was quite outstanding, as was its top speed of nearly 90 mph.

In spite of its small size, (it rarely built even 1,000 cars in a year) Alvis, was always technically ambitious, so the Speed Twenty was improved significantly in four years. By 1933 not only was there a new chassis with independent front suspension, but also a modern synchromesh gearbox, both these features being years ahead of other British mass-market concerns.

All this, of course, came at a price, for the original Speed Twenty cost £695, while later saloons cost up to £850. Even so, by producing 1,165 examples, Alvis made the Speed Twenty its highest-selling pre-war car, during which time there were four sub-types, all of them with triple SU carburettor engines. By the mid 1930s, with the Speed Twenty reaching maturity, Alvis cars had become progressively larger, so the next generation of six-cylinder engines had 3.5-litre engines, and aimed for an even more rarified market than before.

Alvis Speed Twenty

Years in production: 1932–35
Structure: Front engine/rear-drive. Separate chassis
Engine type: 6-cylinder, overhead-valve
Bore and stroke: 73 x 100 mm
Capacity: 2,511 cc
Power: 87 bhp @ 4,000 rpm
Fuel supply: Three horizontal SU carburettors
Suspension: Beam-axle front, beam-axle rear
Weight: 2,912 lb
Top speed: 89 mph

Below: This was always a low-slung car with impeccable road manners, and (depending on the body style chosen) a variety of attractive styling. The whole car was led by that characteristic red triangular radiator badge.

1932 Ford 8 hp Model Y

If the Model T Ford was vital to Ford-USA's future, the Ford 8 hp Model Y was the single model which set Ford-UK on the way to market leadership. It was Ford's first truly small car, their cheapest-ever car, and it opened up Ford motoring to the masses.

Until the 1930s, Ford-UK's fortune was tied up in the assembly of American models such as the Model T and the Model A. The building of a new factory at Dagenham, in Essex, and the onset of the Depression in Europe made Ford desperate for something smaller, cheaper – and domestic. Although the Model Y was British-made, it was engineered and styled entirely in the USA. Those were the days when Ford ruled its world-wide empire from Dearborn, near Detroit, with a rod of iron. Every part of the car – the chassis, the tiny side-valve engine, and its style, came from the other side of the Atlantic.

The result was a car whose blood lines were still in evidence at Ford until the end of the 1950s, when the last of the Popular models was built. In 27 years, all the cars in this family were based on the same simple chassis frame, with transverse-leaf spring suspension on front and rear beam-axles, and with a version of the side-valve engine. Early Model Ys boasted 933 cc and 23 bhp, while the last, definitive units had 1,172 cc and 36 bhp.

Sold from mid-1932 as a cheap and cheerful two-door (Tudor) saloon for little more than £120, the Model Y immediately carved out a 40 per cent share of the 8 hp market, which had hitherto been dominated by the Morris Minor and the Austin Seven. The Model Y was so outstanding that when the Minor was renewed, it was replaced by a clone of the small Ford.

Model Ys provided marginal motoring at a very low cost, with tiny maintenance costs from an expanding line of Ford dealerships; nothing was allowed to push up the price. Four-door saloons soon joined the range, and there were specials from outside coachbuilders. The high point (the low point, really, in pricing terms) was when the stripped-out Popular of 1935 was launched, at a retail price of only £100 – the first time this had ever been achieved for a British series-production saloon.

The Model Y was slow, it only had a three-speed gearbox, and it had a tendency to wander from side to side on the road as its suspension flexed, but (like the Model T which preceded it), it provided unbeatable value and ample space for a complete family. Nearly 158,000 were produced in five years, before the re-styled and somewhat larger Model C 8 hp and 10 hp Fords took over in 1937. In that short time a principle had been established, which continues to this day in the current Ford range.

Right: This was Ford's first truly small car, their cheapest-ever which opened up Ford motoring to the masses with the bloodline of its design still in evidence until the end of the 1950s with the Ford Anglia and Ford Prefect.

Ford 8 hp Model Y

Years in production: 1932–37
Structure: Front engine/rear-drive
Separate chassis
Engine type: 4-cylinder, side-valve
Bore and stroke: 56.6 x 92.5 mm
Capacity: 933 cc
Power: 23 bhp @ 4,000 rpm
Fuel supply: One downdraught
Zenith carburettor
Suspension: Beam-axle front,
beam-axle rear
Weight: 1,484 lb
Top speed: 59 mph

1933 Aston Martin Le Mans

The first Aston Martin cars were built in 1922, but the marque had a chequered financial record for many years. Prices were high and sales were low, because of the cars' specialised nature, and because the business was small.

There were several important changes of management in the first decade of production, and stability was finally established when Sir Arthur Sutherland took control in 1932. The well-liked four single overhead camshaft engine appeared in 1927, and would be used in one form or another for the next ten years. At the same time 'Bert' Bertelli rejuvenated the company, putting the cars into important races with considerable success.

The Sports and International models were established from 1927, but were costly to build. With the company fast fading away, Sir Arthur introduced revised cars, using bought-in proprietary components to reduce costs, and with a new chassis frame. The result was the launch of the new International and Le Mans models which sold steadily and consistently for the next two years.

The latest cars combined a new chassis frame, developed versions of the overhead-camshaft engine, and a proprietary Moss transmission, with a choice of wheelbase lengths and body styles. The Le Mans (so named after the team's motorsport appearances) was closely related to the new International, but had a lowered radiator, slab fuel tank, and chassis modifications.

Compared with the multitude of mundane engines offered by other makers, the Aston Martin's single-cam was not only efficient – 70 bhp from 1.5 litres was outstanding by early 1930s standards – but well specified, and was prepared to run for ever. Until 1932 an International Le Mans had sold (very slowly!) for £650, while the latest (1933) model retailed at £595.

Aston Martin was so encouraged by the car's reception that they made haste to offer alternative wheelbase lengths – of 102 in/2591 mm or 120 in/3048 cc – in future seasons, with a choice of open two-seater of four-seater bodywork. Long, low, and immediately recognisable by their unique radiator style, these cars had great character, riding hard, but making all the appropriate mechanical noises. They were exclusive too, for in 1932 and 1933, only 130 Aston Martins of all types were produced. Although the marque name survived, later, post-war, Aston Martins were completely different.

Aston Martin Le Mans

Years in production: 1932–33
Structure: Front engine/rear-drive Separate chassis
Engine type: 4-cylinder, single overhead camshaft
Bore and stroke: 69.3 x 99 mm
Capacity: 1,495 cc
Power: 70 bhp @ 4,750 rpm
Fuel supply: Two horizontal SU carburettors
Suspension: Beam-axle front, beam-axle rear
Weight: 2,128 lb
Top speed: 85 mph

Below and above: By the standards of the early 1930s, these were not only speedy cars (the Le Mans' top speed was about 85 mph which compared well with the pace of the cheaper MG and Singer sports cars of the day), but were also significantly cheaper than before, retailing at £595.

1933 Bentley 3½-litre

Although the legendary 'W.O.' Bentley cars built a fine reputation in a mere ten years, they were not a commercial success, so after the company had run through at least three tranches of capital, it went broke for the last time in 1931. After a rather sordid courtroom battle, Bentley was bought up by Rolls-Royce, and re-developed in its own image. There was a two year hiatus, while the last surviving 'W.O.' cars were bodied and sold off, and a new model was developed.

The cars which appeared in 1933 shared only a radiator badge with their earlier namesakes. Marketed under the banner of the 'Silent Sports Car', the first 'Rolls-Bentley' (or 'Derby Bentley') was the 3½-litre model of 1933, which leaned heavily on the existing Rolls-Royce 20/25 model for its running gear. The two cars, however, had little in common. Although they shared the same basic 3.7-litre six-cylinder engine, that used in the Bentley was much-modified and more powerful (we were never told how powerful, though). This was used with the Rolls-Royce transmission in a new chassis which, in spite of what the traditionalists might say, was much lighter and more capable than ever before.

Bentley 3½ litre

Years in production: 1933–36
Structure: Front engine/rear-drive
Separate chassis
Engine type: 6-cylinder, overhead-valve
Bore and stroke: 88.9 x 114.3 mm
Capacity: 3,669 cc
Power: Never revealed
Fuel supply: Two horizontal SU carburettors
Suspension: Beam-axle front, beam-axle rear
Weight: 3,920 lb
Top speed: 95 mph

The new Bentleys were bodied by independent coachbuilders, a good proportion being clothed by Park Ward, Barker and Gurney Nutting, each producing noticeably more rakish styles than anything normally committed to a Rolls-Royce base. Although prices crept up in the years which followed, an early 3½-litre would cost about £1,500 to put on the road – a price which one should compare with the £100 Ford 8 hp saloon of the period.

To call it a 'sports car', would stretch the point, but this new Bentley was certainly a fast and capable 'grand tourer'. A 90 mph top speed, which was

Below and left: The new Bentleys were fast, capable of a top speed of 90 mph. These were light and appealing cars, sharing the same radiator badge as the 'W.O.' Bentleys.

normal for these original cars, was very fast by the standards of the day. The Bentley's character, too, was very light and appealing, something proved by the hundreds of cars which still survive.

As competition increased, and as the weight of the cars inexorably crept up, more performance was needed, so from 1936, the 4¼-litre model took over (with a 4,257 cc engine), while a four-speed 'overdrive' gearbox was standardised from 1938, though none ever achieved 100 mph in standard coachwork form. By the summer of 1939 the range was at the height of its fame, and its replacement by a brand new generation Rolls–Bentley was only prevented by the outbreak of the Second World War with Hitler's Germany.

In six years nearly 2,500 Bentleys were produced, 1,191 of them the original 3½-litre types.

1936 Rolls-Royce Phantom III

Looking back over the decades, one has to ask what inspired Rolls-Royce to build a car as complex as the Phantom III, for this was the very first British car which had ever been designed around a V12 engine. Logically, however, one can see that Rolls-Royce had to compete with Hispano-Suiza, who also had a V12, and particularly with Cadillac, who were selling limited numbers of V16-engined machines. In the most discreet way, too, there must also have been a good marketing reason to supplement the efforts of the aircraft engine division, which had just started building the famous V12 Merlin engine, which would power the Spitfires, Hurricanes, Lancasters and Mosquitoes of the RAF in the Second World War.

As the successor of the existing company flagship, the Phantom II, the new Rolls-Royce was entitled Phantom III. Although no larger than before, it had a new chassis frame, complete with independent front suspension (which had been copied very carefully from the latest General Motors layouts), but all other mechanical attention was centred on the V12 engine. Not only was this a real leviathan, at 7.34 litres, but it also featured hydraulic tappets ('valve lifters', as Americans always called them), and was more powerful than any previous Rolls-Royce engine. It needed to be, for the coachbuilt machines could be extremely heavy, and they carried such craggy bodywork with a vast frontal area that top speeds were rarely more than 90 mph.

Most owners, it has to be said, were far more interested in buying a car in which they could not even hear the engine running, and in which they could luxuriate in total comfort.

To their shame (though the news rarely got out at the time), Rolls-Royce found that these engines were troublesome (particularly if the new tappets got sludge in their mechanisms), so there were no long-term plans to improve the power unit in the 1940s. The advent of war, and the post-war chance to start again, must have been a relief, although another consequence was that very few V12-engined Phantom IIIs survive into the classic car era. Only 710 were ever built.

Rolls-Royce Phantom III

Years in production: 1936–39
Structure: Front engine/rear-drive
Separate chassis
Engine type: V12-cylinder, overhead-valve
Bore and stroke: 82.5 x 114.3 mm
Capacity: 7,338 cc
Power: Never officially revealed
Fuel supply: Single downdraught carburettor
Suspension: Independent front, beam-axle rear
Weight: 5,400 lb
Top speed: 90 mph

Right: The Rolls-Royce Phantom III – if one had to ask the price, one could probably not afford it, for these were the most exclusive and expensive of all late-1930s British motor cars.

1935 Hillman Minx

A motor car does not have to be beautiful or incredibly fast, to become a classic. It must, above all, stand out as a great example of what was right for its day. Just as there were important sports cars between the wars, so were there also commercially successful family cars. The Hillman Minx of 1935–39 was one of them.

Until 1928, Hillman had been independent, but following its purchase by Rootes Ltd (motor traders and distributors whose guiding light was 'Billy' Rootes, of Maidstone), it was rapidly turned into a mass production concern. Along with Humber, it became a major constituent part of the Rootes Group, which immediately became one of the British 'big six' car makers.

The original, and all-new Minx was previewed in 1931, and went on sale in 1932, but it was the second-generation Minx (the 'Minx Magnificent', as its bonnet badge advertised) which finally established the type. From then until the 1970s, there would always be a Hillman Minx in the Rootes Group line-up.

Mechanically it was conventional, with a separate chassis, beam-axle front and rear suspensions, and a side-valve engine, but there was interest in the detail, and it may be significant that both Bill Heynes (later legendary at Jaguar) and Alec Issigonis (of Mini fame) were both employed at Rootes at this time.

The most popular version was a rounded four-door saloon (Pressed Steel supplied the bodies), but a few limited-edition styles were also produced. It was neither fast (the top speed was about 60 mph), nor temperamental, but it was reliable, refined by the standards of the 1930s, and roomy enough to carry four or even five adults.

More than all this, a Minx was remarkably cheap, for in 1935 British prices started at a mere £159. No wonder the first 10,000 were built in a matter of months, or that a total of 92,095 cars were built in only four full years and the side-valve engine itself would be used in Rootes Group cars until 1957.

Hillman Minx

Years in production: (Second generation car) 1935–39
Structure: Front engine/rear-drive. Separate chassis
Engine type: 4-cylinder, side-valve
Bore and stroke: 63 x 95 mm
Capacity: 1,185 cc
Power: 30 bhp @ 4,100 rpm
Fuel supply: One downdraught Solex carburettor
Suspension: Beam-axle front and rear
Weight: 2,130 lb
Top speed: 60 mph

Above: Built in large quantities in Coventry, it was the highest-selling Rootes Group car of the day, and eventually donated its running gear to more up-market machines such as the Talbot Tens of the period.

1936 MG TA

The watershed of MG's early years came in 1935, when the company's guardian, Lord Nuffield, transferred its ownership to his vast new Nuffield Organisation. At the same time, his managing director, Len Lord, decreed that future MG sports cars should use many more off-the-shelf components than before.

One early result was the launch of the TA, the first of a long and successful line of T-series cars, which launched MG even faster down the road to world-wide fame. Longer, wider, heavier, but simpler than the PB model which it replaced, the TA was a classic MG sports car.

Although it was built around a simple ladder-style chassis frame, and had a body shell assembled around a wooden frame – both of which were traditional MG in every way – the TA's real innovation as far as the customers were concerned was in its engine and transmission. For the first time in eight years, this was an MG without an overhead-camshaft engine, and it was also the first to have a synchromesh (as opposed to a 'crash') gearbox.

The TA, in fact, had been laid out in the Nuffield design offices, where the engineers had chosen to use modified versions of the latest Morris/Wolseley engines and running gear. According to the traditionalists (who were wrong) this ruined the MG's character, but Nuffield's planners produced a car that was simpler, faster, and more reliable than before. Before long, the TA was selling faster than any previous MG, and only one look at its style spelt out the reason. Here was a two-seater car with all the established MG virtues of sweeping front wings, proud free-standing headlamps, and an unmistakable radiator grille. Not only that, but it was probably the first Midget to have a cockpit large enough for two adults.

Although the 1,292 cc engine was neither as specialised, nor as high-revving, as its predecessors, it delivered the goods, for this was the fastest Midget yet. In some ways it was almost an embarrassment for MG, as it was also little slower than the six-cylinder Magnettes, which were still available.

With the virtues came all the expected failings – a rock-hard ride, sensitive steering, sketchy all-weather equipment, and a tendency to leak water in heavy rainstorms – but no-one seemed to care. Like earlier Midgets, this was a car with a heart and soul, which seemed to relate to every owner's yearnings.

The TA set MG on a new sports car path, for the re-engined TB took over successfully in 1939, and the TC (a lightly-modified TB) would be a huge success in the late 1940s. It was a very important Midget: before the arrival of the TA, MG's commercial future had been in doubt, but afterwards the subject was never mentioned again.

MG TA

Years in production: 1936–39
Structure: Front engine/rear-drive. Separate chassis
Engine type: 4-cylinder, overhead-valve
Bore and stroke: 63.5 x 102 mm
Capacity: 1,292 cc
Power: 50 bhp @ 4,500 rpm
Fuel supply: Two horizontal SU carburettors
Suspension: Beam-axle front, beam-axle rear
Weight: 1,765 lb
Top speed: 78 mph

Below and above: The TA sold faster than any earlier MG. It was a simple, fast and reliable two-seater with the famous MG badge displayed prominently above its distinctive radiator grill.

1936 SS-Jaguar SS100

SS and SS-Jaguar came from nowhere to lead the middle class car market, during the 1930s, which was a credit to William Lyons and his single-minded enterprise. Whereas the original 1932 SS1 had used humble side-valve Standard engines, late 1930s SS-Jaguars had powerful, purpose-designed overhead-valve 'sixes'. That, and a line-up of elegant styles, made them extremely desirable.

New for 1936, the SS-Jaguars had four-cylinder and six-cylinder engines, saloon and drop-head coupé body styles, along with one very special derivative – the rakish two-seater SS100 sports car. Using a short wheelbase version of the touring cars' chassis, but with the same engines, transmissions and other running gear, the SS100 was a wickedly attractive two-seater which came as close to sex-on-wheels as its descendant the E-type a quarter of a century later.

Running on a 102 in/2591 mm wheelbase chassis, with hard beam-axle suspension and rather heavy and imprecise steering, the SS100 did not even attempt to give its occupants a peaceful ride, but inspired excitement at every turn. Its sweeping front wings were dominated by huge headlamps; the bonnet was long, low, and covered in louvres; the engine bay was full of impressive power, while the rear wings were abbreviated and rather coquettishly curved. Cutaway doors, a slab fuel tank, and a fold-down windscreen all added to this car's irresistible visual appeal.

Original SS100s had 2.7-litre engines, a 95 mph top speed, and cost £395, but from 1938 there was the option of a 125 bhp/ 3,485 cc power unit, from which 101 mph was available, all for a mere £445. There was much petty jealousy from SS-Jaguar's rivals, but none of them could counter the colossal (by 1930s standards) performance, the eye-catching looks, or the amazing value-for-money pricing.

The fact that sales were so limited – only 198 2.5-litre and 116 3.5-litre types were produced in four years – reflected the heavy annual taxation of the period, rather than the car's limitations. It was, admittedly, one of those machines one only ever bought as a 'toy' (there was virtually nowhere to stow baggage, and rather sketchy all-weather accommodation), but its excitement-per-pound rating must have been one of the most impressive of all time.

SS-Jaguar considered making a closed two-seater coupé version of the same car, but this never progressed beyond a single prototype. In the more sober motoring period which followed the Second World War, there was no place for an SS100 in the line-up, but the vast majority of these machines seem to have survived.

SS-Jaguar SS100

Years in production: 1936–39
Structure: Front engine/rear-drive. Separate chassis
Engine type: 6-cylinder, overhead-valve
Bore and stroke: 73 x 106 mm/82 x 110 mm
Capacity: 2,663 cc/3,485 cc
Power: 102 bhp @ 4,600 rpm/125 bhp @ 4,250 rpm
Fuel supply: Two horizontal SU carburettors
Suspension: Beam-axle front, beam-axle rear
Weight: 2,576 lb
Top speed: 94/101 mph

Below and right: Very appealing with its long bonnet, huge head–lamps and cutaway doors, the SS100 was a car of impressive power and excitement as well as being good value for money.

1937 Lagonda V12

Those who didn't know that the extremely desirable Lagonda V12 was inspired by W.O. Bentley could surely have guessed, for here was a massive, locomotive-like machine, with an engine producing immense torque, and all the characteristics of the legendary 'vintage' Bentleys. Those cars, at least, had carried the famous badge, but the Lagonda V12 was a latter-day 'W.O.' by another name.

Bentley himself, the confident and renowned engineer, had been tied to Rolls-Royce since the take-over of 1931, but was eventually released in 1935, after which he immediately joined the small Lagonda company, which made its cars at Staines, in Middlesex. Current Lagondas of the early 1930s were worthy but rather rough sports and saloon cars, which used massive Meadows six-cylinder engines. Bentley's new team quickly refined what they found, developed a new chassis, and finally set about the design of a new engine, an ambitiously-detailed 4.5-litre V12. Although the prototype was shown at the Olympia Motor Show of 1936, it was still not complete, and production units were not delivered until 1938.

Lagonda V12

Years in production: 1937–39
Structure: Front engine/rear-drive. Separate chassis
Engine type: V12-cylinder, single overhead-camshaft
Bore and stroke: 75 x 84.5 mm
Capacity: 4,480 cc
Power: 180 bhp @ 5,500 rpm
Fuel supply: Two downdraught Solex carburettors
Suspension: Independent front, beam-axle rear
Weight: 4,440 lb
Top speed: 101 mph

The V12's chassis was solid, well detailed, and modern. It shared many of the various body styles with the LG6 type (Meadows six-cylinder-engined) which ran alongside it, so all attention was concentrated on the engine. This was only the second British V12 to go on sale (Rolls-Royce, with the Phantom III having the first), though Hispano-Suiza also had such a power unit. It had an overhead-camshaft valve gear and 'two of everything' – SU carburettors, electrical coils and fuel pumps – so this was a smooth and effective power unit, which not only produced 180 bhp, but was the most powerful of all pre-war British engines.

Available in saloon, drop-head coupé, limousine, tourer and other derivatives, each and every V12 had to be hand-built – and in fact only 189 were built before war broke out.

The engine went on to have a fine career in light naval craft, but was not revived after the war.

Below: Undeniably expensive cars, (from £1,550 in 1938, at a time when the Bentley 4.25-litre cost only £1,430), they were bound to sell slowly, but because every type had a top speed of more than 100 mph, they were very popular.

1937 Triumph Dolomite Roadster

Donald Healey might not have been a trained engineer, or a trained stylist, but he always managed to inspire his teams to produce exceptional cars. The distinctively shaped Triumph Dolomite Roadster was a fine example.

Already famous for winning the Monte Carlo Rally in 1931, Donald Healey joined Triumph in 1933, soon rising to become the company's technical director. Having been allowed one expensive indulgence, which was the supercharged Dolomite Straight Eight, he then up-graded Triumph's production car range of Glorias and Vitesses. The arrival of a new Dolomite range (no relation) denoted the launch of a new family of four- and six-cylinder engines.

One feature of the new Dolomites in 1936 was their 'waterfall' style of radiator grille, which stylist Walter Belgrove had produced as an obvious inspiration from the latest Hudson Terraplanes. This was distinctive enough, but when added to the style of body which appeared in 1938, it produced a real effect. Well trimmed and furnished, the Dolomite Roadster, which was produced in very limited numbers,

Triumph Dolomite Roadster

Years in production: 1937–39
Structure: Front engine/rear-drive. Separate chassis
SPEC. FOR 2-LITRE
Engine type: 6-cylinder, over head-valve
Bore and stroke: 65 x 100 mm
Capacity: 1,991 cc
Power: 75 bhp @ 4,500 rpm
Fuel supply: Three horizontal SU carburettors
Suspension: Beam-axle front, beam-axle rear
Weight: 3,304 lb
Top speed: 80 mph

was more 'drop-head' than 'roadster', and it was available in two forms: a four-cylinder 1,767 cc type, or a six-cylinder 1,991 cc model with a longer (and even more elegant) wheelbase. On this body the waterfall grille was matched to a two-seater front compartment, and a long sweeping tail concealed a lift-up panel which hid two further 'dickey' seats. Although this was already an obsolete feature, and the whole thing was a trifle over-the-top, it was striking, and attractive.

When the six-cylinder engine was fitted, the top speed was around 80 mph, enough to make it a useful rally car. For the well-to-do middle class sportsman, who could choose between Triumph, SS-Jaguar, Riley, MG and other substantial cars, this was an intriguing contender and, at £450 for the 116 in/2,946 mm wheelbase version, it was good value.

Seat trim was in pigskin-grained leather, winding windows were provided in the doors, there was a disappearing front arm rest between the seats, and discreet steps were fitted to allow access to the dickey seats, for which there were no doors. In the rather genteel British motoring competitions of the day it was a sure-fire contender for Concours awards.

Elegant by the standards of the day, it died at the outbreak of war, for post-war Triumphs were really modified Standards, and a new-generation Roadster was not nearly as smart as the original.

Below and right: Distinguished by the 'waterfall' style of its radiator grille, the Dolomite Roadster had a sweeping tail which concealed a lift-up panel with two middle 'dickey' seats.

The superb radiator grill and huge headlamps contributed to the eye catching looks of the 1936 SS100 Jaguar.

The Classic Years

1945–1970

Morgan 4/4 ✪ Riley RM Series ✪ Allard Sports Car
Jowett Javelin ✪ Jaguar XK120 ✪ Land-Rover ✪ Morris Minor
Bond Minicar 3-wheeler ✪ Healey Silverstone ✪ Dellow Sports Car
Rover P4 ✪ Ford Consul/Zephyr Six ✪ MG TD
Standard Vanguard ✪ Bentley Continental R-Type ✪ Triumph TR2
MG MGA ✪ Armstrong-Siddeley Star Sapphire ✪ Austin-Healey Sprite
Lotus Elite ✪ Triumph Herald ✪ Austin-Healey 3000
Austin-Morris Mini ✪ Jaguar 3.8 Mk II
Jaguar E-Type ✪ AC Cobra ✪ Aston Martin DB5 ✪ Hillman Imp
Sunbeam Tiger ✪ Jensen FF & Interceptor ✪ Range Rover

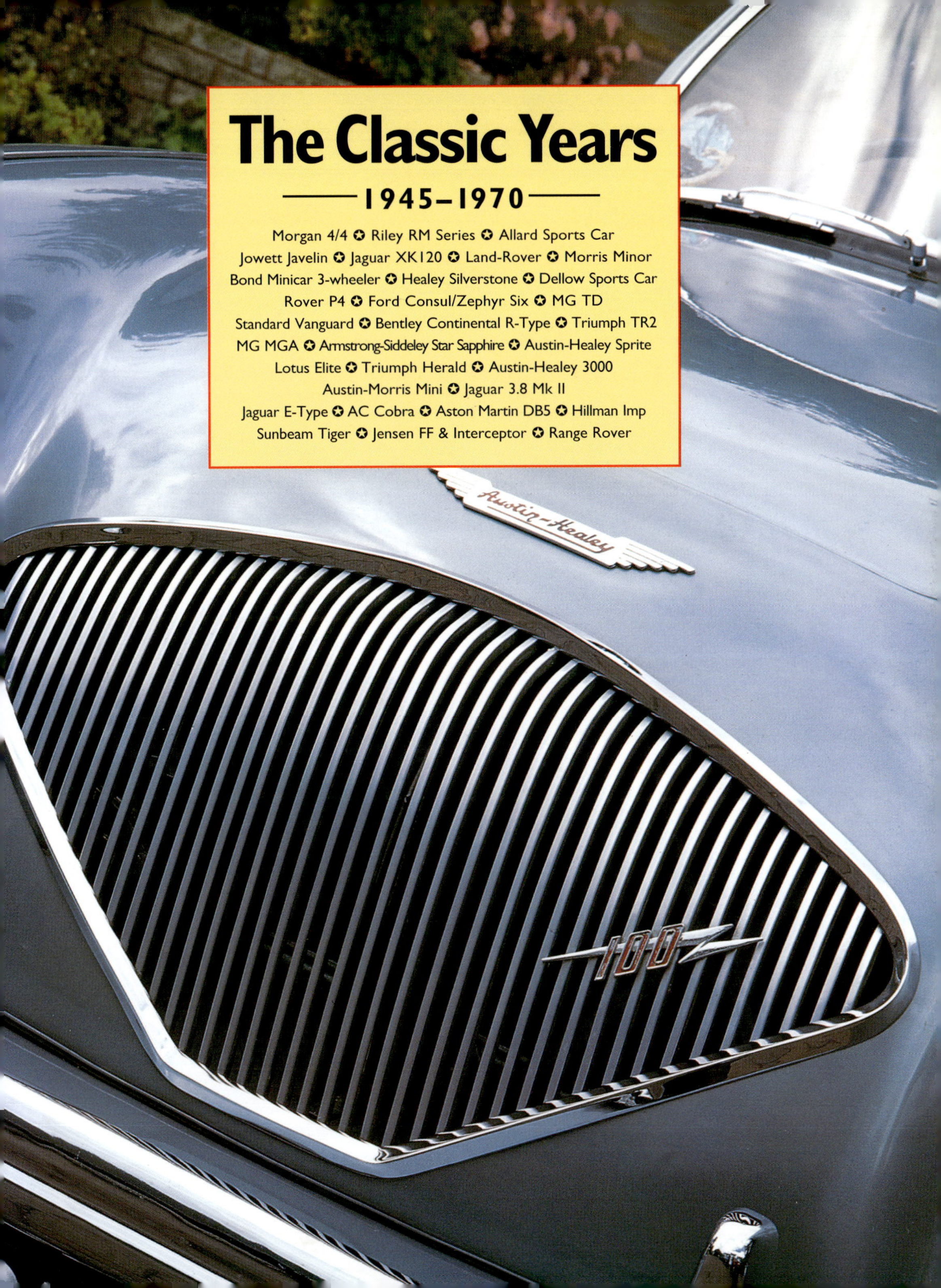

The Classic Years

For Britain's motor industry, the Second World War changed everything. When Britain's car makers returned to their peacetime businesses in 1945, they faced a different reality. The market-place, clientele, social climate and economy had all been transformed.

It was not only the factories which built the cars, but also the nations and the individual customers who bought them which had been badly battered by the fighting; furthermore, prices had more than doubled in six years. In order to raise revenue, the British government (almost bankrupt by the sheer cost of the war) had introduced a purchase tax on what they defined as luxury items – which naturally included cars. Even so, if economic conditions had not then been turned on their heads, British car makers might still have been able to carry on where they left off in 1939.

A Labour government took over for the first time since 1931, a government which indulged in an orgy of nationalisation, raised taxes to pay for this, followed a long-term policy of austerity, and kept rationing of everything from bread to petrol going for years longer than was really justified. There was a shortage of all materials (and national reconstruction had the utmost priority), and it was obviously going to take years to bring truly new post-war cars to the market. To fill the gap, therefore, the motor industry mostly re-started by building mildly up-dated versions of their 1939 models.

HUGE DEMAND

After six years in which private car production had ceased, and in which many older cars had been worn out, abandoned or destroyed, there was a huge demand for new cars all over the world. Almost any car, however old-fashioned, or crudely developed, found sales in the first post-war years.

Until the 1950s, therefore, Britain's motor industry thrived in this climate. Although a government recommendation for car makers to follow a 'one-model policy' never really took off, a new type of flat-rate taxation influenced the architecture of future engines, and an 'export or die' philosophy obliged companies to export most of their output (strictly monitored steel supply quotas saw to that). This meant that British customers had to join huge waiting lists, and originally had to sign

Below: After crossing the Atlantic from New York in the liner Queen Elizabeth, a Rolls-Royce Silver Cloud is re-fuelled by a three-wheel Scammell Esso transporter at Southampton dockside in 1960.

Above: In 1966 an E-Type Jaguar Coupé was regarded as the height of fashion, driven by pop and film stars; its enduring beauty means it can still turn heads today.

'covenants' to stop them re-selling recently delivered new cars for profit on to a black market. Cars were only available to priority customers at first (doctors and other 'essential workers' among them). For the private individual, new cars ordered in 1946 would often not arrive until the early 1950s, sometimes to an entirely different and later specification.

For the motor industry, this was a financial golden age, and several car makers became complacent about their future. Only one large merger (of Austin with the Nuffield Organisation in 1952, to form BMC) took place, and this was never pursued to its logical conclusion. Aston Martin also merged with Lagonda, but this was at the expensive end of the market, and was less significant.

To satisfy the demand on their own terms, and with new export opportunities, the 'big five' car makers churned out more and more conventional machinery. Insatiable demand and great enthusiasm from private owners, however, encouraged the production of new styles and ranges. Thoughtful companies like Rover went into a new market sector with the Land Rover, old-fashioned types such as Jowett (with the Javelin and the Jupiter) sought to change their image, while thrusting businesses like Jaguar set up entirely new ranges (such as the XK120 sports cars and the Mk VII saloons). They were joined by brash new makes such as Allard, Bristol, Healey and Lotus, who used different materials where there was no steel, ingenuity instead of conventional engineering where there was an opportunity, and crossed fingers where there was a lack of finance.

Among the mass-producers, some designers were allowed to look into the future, and it wasn't long before modern cars (which have subsequently become known as 'classics' began to appear. The bulbous Morris Minor of 1948 set new small-car standards, if not of performance, then certainly in chassis behaviour; the Consul/Zephyr series from Ford introduced a whole list of technical novelties, while the Rootes Group (Hillman, Humber and Sunbeam) developed the art of product planning (or squeezing many models out of restricted resources).

NEW ENTERPRISE

The big advances in styling, engineering and sheer motoring excitement came from the independent makers. If they could not buy sheet steel, they made do with aluminium, with steel tubes and with fibreglass. Smaller companies were early innovators; they were the first to exploit aerospace construction such as multi-tube space frames and disc brakes, and were always ready to pioneer strange aerodynamic shapes or materials to make their point. An AC, an Allard, a Bristol, or even a Bond three-wheeler might not appeal to everyone – but they were available and they all had their merits.

Then, in the 1950s, came the boom in British sports cars. MG and Jaguar, both well-established, blossomed with new types, while Austin-Healey, Triumph and Sunbeam all joined in. Though staid car makers like Alvis, Jowett and Daimler all tried to surf this tidal wave, they failed, and one of the few new companies to become permanently established was Colin Chapman's Lotus. North America, in particular, loved Britain's TR2s, MGAs, Alpines and Austin-Healey 100s, but that love-affair became even more intense in the 1960s with the arrival of small sports cars like the Triumph Spitfire, the Austin-Healey Sprite, MG Midget and the sensational Jaguar E-type.

This, if only the pundits had known it, was really the start of the now-recognised 'classic' era, where individual motor cars of all types became available at amazingly attractive prices. The appeal of sports cars was obvious, but Britain also produced fascinating new models such as the famous front-wheel-drive BMC Mini, and technically interesting cars such as the Triumph Herald and the Hillman Imp.

Yet this was not before time, as Europe's car makers had made a strong recovery from the devastation of war, and had always produced more interesting cars than the British. Say what you like about the looks of the VW Beetle, or of the crudities of the Fiat 600 and Renault Dauphine types, they sold in vast quantities, and quite overshadowed many British machines.

RATIONALISATION

Much of the romance of making motor cars was squeezed out of Britain's industry in the 1960s as a wave of mergers and many transatlantic methods swept through the workshops. Ford and Vauxhall both prospered under American ownership, and were joined by the Rootes Group, who fell to Chrysler.

Standard-Triumph was taken over by Leyland (the truck maker with big ideas) in 1961, who eventually swallowed up Rover and Alvis too. BMC, complacent as ever, thought they were above all this, though they bought up Jaguar just to be sure. Then, in 1968, government pressure saw Leyland merge with BMC-Jaguar, producing the ill-fated British Leyland combine.

Jaguar, Lotus and Aston-Martin-Lagonda were almost the only survivors of the famous old marques. Many fell by the wayside and the roll-call of the vanished makes was heartbreaking: Allard, Alvis, Armstrong-Siddeley, Healey, Invicta, Jowett, Lea-Francis and many others all closed their doors, and worse was to follow. Although the industry closed ranks, concentrating on fewer and fewer groups, British car production continued to rise – from 522,515 units in 1950 to 1,352,728 in 1960, and onwards to 1,640,966 in 1970, but this wasn't all unblemished good news. In the same period, imports of foreign cars rocketed from 1,375 in 1950 to 157,956 in 1970, and this was only the beginning.

Rationalisation, expansion and sheer caution meant that cars like the Ford Cortina, the Morris 1100, the

Below: The new Ford Anglia de Luxe 1959/60 with an aerodynamic body tested in wind tunnels. The car featured a unique reverse angle rear screen. It is fondly remembered by many as the car chosen for summer holiday hire in the early 1960s.

Above: The Aston Martin Lagonda DB6 Mk2. This new-look Aston Martin had fuel injection and DBS safety features. It first went on sale on August 21, 1969.

Hillman Minx and the Vauxhall Viva sold in large numbers, and truly interesting and inspiring cars (particularly sports cars) languished in the shadows. Yet it was still Britain's most individual cars from Lotus, Jensen, Range Rover and Austin-Healey which made all the headlines.

It was at this point that motoring history began to repeat itself. In the 1930s observers had tired of the cars currently on offer, had looked back longingly to the cars of the 1920s and started calling them 'vintage'. In the early 1970s many enthusiasts harked back to the 1950s and 1960s, sad that such individualism seemed to have gone for ever. In the 1930s, traditionalists had yearned for a 'vintage' car, but now, having settled on a new definition, they wanted a 'classic'. They didn't really need to know that a dictionary defined classic as being, 'of acknowledged excellence; outstandingly important; remarkably typical...' – for they knew that already, and this was the sort of motor car they wanted to remember from the period.

DOOM AND GLOOM

It was almost by accident that the 'classic car' movement was founded at the same time as the first energy crisis erupted, and it was almost coincidental that the most enterprising of British (and overseas, for that matter) car makers began to pull in their horns at the same time. Britain's original *Classic Cars* magazine was first published in 1973 as inflation soared out of control, as the miners struck, putting the lights out, and as British Leyland became a national joke.

Faced with the threat of petrol rationing, of open-road speed limits almost everywhere (West German autobahns being a notable exception), and of more and more performance- and character-sapping legislation, many motorists feared that all the world's best cars might already have been built. Companies as big as Ford started cancelling sporty models and withdrawing temporarily from motorsport, and all except the brave started developing bigger and better safety bumpers, ever-more varieties of economical engines, and continued to worry about safety regulations.

Only the most optimistic drivers thought that the most exciting cars were still to come. So, what if our sports cars were rapidly losing their markets in the USA, and so what if we were faced with paying a lot more money for our cars in the 1980s? We could still look back on this Golden Age ....

1946 Morgan 4/4

Although the original four-wheeler Morgan was shown in the mid-1930s, it was overshadowed by the company's older three-wheeler models until the end of the Second World War. From that point, while altering the original style only slightly as the years passed by, Morgan concentrated on their four-wheeler sports cars.

Morgans were first made by a family-owned business in 1910 (a situation which has never changed), and even

the first cars employed a type of sliding-pillar independent front suspension which is still used to this day. Assembly was always by hand, always at a leisurely pace, and even in the post-war years it was a good week which saw more than ten complete cars leave the gates in Malvern Link.

The post-war 4/4 retained the simple ladder-style chassis and the rock-hard suspension for which the

Morgan 4/4

Years in production: 1945–50
Structure: Front engine/rear-drive. Separate chassis
Engine type: 4-cylinder, overhead-valve
Bore and stroke: 63.5 x 100 mm
Capacity: 1,267 cc
Power: 40 bhp @ 4,300 rpm
Fuel supply: One downdraught Solex carburettor
Suspension: Independent front, beam-axle rear
Weight: 1,590 lb
Top speed: 77 mph

and even in the post-war years it was a good week which saw more than ten complete cars leave the gates in Malvern Link.

The post-war 4/4 retained the simple ladder-style chassis and the rock-hard suspension for which the marque is noted, and still looked like its 1939 predecessor. It used to be said that the ride was so hard that if one drove over a penny in the road, a skilled driver would know whether 'heads' or 'tails' was uppermost. Although pre-war cars had been powered by Coventry-Climax, the post-war chassis was exclusively fitted with a specially-manufactured overhead-valve Standard 1,267 cc engine (which never appeared in Standard or Triumph models). Although this engine only produced 40 bhp, the Morgan was such a light car that it could reach 75 mph, while handling in a way that made all MG Midget owners jealous.

The style was what we must now call 'traditional Morgan' – it was a low-slung two-seater with sweeping front wings, and free-standing headlamps, along with cutaway doors and the sort of weather protection which made one drive quickly for home in a shower, rather than stop to wrestle with its sticks and removable panels. Up front, there was a near-vertical radiator, flanked by free-standing headlamps, while the coil spring/vertical-pillar front suspension was easily visible from the nose. Most 4/4s were open-top two-seaters, though a more completely trimmed and equipped two-seater drophead coupé (with wind-up windows in the doors) was also available. Bodies were framed from unprotected wood members, with steel or aluminium skin panels tacked into place, and were all manufactured in the Morgan factory.

Here was an old-style, no-compromise sports car made in modern times – a philosophy which Morgan has never abandoned. Requests for a more modern specification were politely shrugged off, waiting lists grew, and Morgan has been financially healthy ever since. Before the 4/4 was replaced by the altogether larger 2.1-litre Plus 4 of 1950, a grand total of 1,720 4/4s were sold.

Left: Hand assembled, these low-slung two-seater sports cars had cutaway doors and a near vertical radiator which was flanked by free-standing headlamps. Most were open topped and had rock-hard suspension.

1946 Riley RM Series

Although Riley of Coventry, whose proud advertising slogan was, 'As Old as the Industry', had hit financial problems in 1938, it was rescued by Lord Nuffield, added to the Nuffield Organisation's quiver of marques, and encouraged to grow again after the Second World War. The new RM (Riley Motors) Series models of the post-war era were a remarkable tribute to that rebirth.

Riley retained the justly famous twin high-camshaft 1.5-litre and 2.5-litre four-cylinder engines as part of the new range, but used them to power a truly sleek, low and stylish family of four-seater saloons, which shared the same cabin, but different wheelbases. With torsion bar independent front suspension and rack-and-pinion steering, the chassis was advanced and effective, and although the body style had only semi-recessed headlamps reminiscent of the 1930s, it was nevertheless elegant and nicely proportioned, with a series of rakish lines.

Riley RM Series

Years in production: 1946–55
Structure: Front engine/rear-drive. Separate chassis
Engine type: 4-cylinder, overhead-valve
SPEC. FOR 2$\frac{1}{2}$-LITRE
Bore and stroke: 80.5 x 120 mm
Capacity: 2,443 cc
Power: 100 bhp @ 4,500 rpm
Fuel supply: Two horizontal SU carburettors
Suspension: Independent front, beam-axle rear
Weight: 3,136 lb
Top speed: 95 mph

The 1½-litre model, which had a top speed of 78 mph, was available first, but it was the 2½-litre model, which not only had a longer wheelbase, but 100 bhp instead of 55 bhp, which caused such a stir. Although the 1½-litre was an appealing sports saloon, it was quite expensive (£710 at first) and not outstandingly fast; the 2½-litre version, on the other hand, was a much more serious proposition. Here was a car which not only had remarkably good handling, and steering so accurate that it made most other British cars of the day look sluggish, but it had a top speed of 95 mph, and was equipped in that typically British combination of wood, leather and carpet which made every owner feel special.

Although traditional Riley enthusiasts did not like to admit it, here was a car which was superior to any Riley

Left and above: Hand-built, these sports cars had aluminium-panelled bodies.

model ever built by the original family concern. The car looked good, behaved impeccably, and it was an easy match for its competition. Later in the 1940s, final assembly was moved from Coventry to the MG factory at Abingdon, and a four-seater convertible version of the original style also appeared, along with a very limited number of three-seater Roadsters, but it was always the saloons which dominated the sales charts.

Finally, in 1953 the 2½-litre car was discontinued (it was replaced by the Nuffield-designed Pathfinder, which was not a good car), though a facelifted Riley 1½-litre continued until 1955. No fewer than 13,950 1½s, and 8,959 2½s, had been made.

1946 Allard Sports Car

The Allard was one of those hand-built, individually-designed sporting cars which flourished briefly after the Second World War, and died away as soon as shortages and waiting lists disappeared. Inspired by London motor trader Sydney Allard, the first 'Allard Specials' were trials cars built in the 1930s, but production of a big, and unmistakably styled road car followed in 1946.

The original Allard was based almost entirely on Ford V8 running gear – chassis, engine, transmission and suspension items – which were modified to suit Syd's own ideas, although the aluminium-panelled bodies (complete with their long, swooping noses) were all his own invention. An Allard, therefore, combined the simplicity and easy availability of Ford parts, with a certain exclusivity, which had a great charm at a time when new cars were scarce. Even by late-1940s standards, the ride, handling and steering were no more than adequate, but the performance was encouraging. Standard Ford side-valve engines produced only 85 bhp, but enlarged (Mercury), more highly-tuned examples were also available to make them into truly fierce machines.

Allard Sports Car
Years in production: 1946–53
Structure: Front engine/rear-drive. Separate chassis
Engine type: V8-cylinder, side-valve
Bore and stroke: 77.8 x 95 mm
Capacity: 3,622 cc
Power: 85 bhp @ 3,800 rpm
Fuel supply: One downdraught Zenith carburettor
Suspension: Independent front, beam-axle rear
Weight: 2,240 lb
Top speed: 85 mph

The first Allard of 1946 was the J1 competition two-seater, which was closely followed by a longer and heavier K-type, while the L-type was a full four-seater tourer. All shared the same type of divided-axle/transverse-leaf spring front suspension, and the same frontal styling.

An early Allard's appeal was not entirely in its performance, nor even in its styling, but in its extrovert character, and its

relatively easy availability. Although an Allard cost as much as a Jaguar XK120, it was simpler to maintain and repair, and the fact that private owners also started winning rallies in it helped enormously.

By the early 1950s massively powerful Cadillac V8-powered J2s and J2Xs (pictured) were on the market, an all-new tubular chassis frame was being designed, and touring Allards like the P1 saloon and the M2X convertible had fleshed out the range. Sydney Allard's famous P1 victory in the 1953 Monte Carlo Rally made many headlines, but Allard's short career was almost over. The last of these V8-engined cars was made in 1955. All in all, about 1,800 of this family were produced.

Above: These were hand-built cars, individually designed but using freely available Ford engine parts. The bodywork was made of aluminium panels and the cars were as expensive as the Jaguar XK120, but easier to maintain and repair.

1947 Jowett Javelin

Few cars are designed by one man, but the Jowett Javelin certainly qualifies for that honour. Although its engine was a flat-four, the entire design was laid out by Gerald Palmer, who had already learned much of his craft at MG and in the Nuffield Organisation.

For far too long, Jowett cars, which were made in Bradford, had been simple, rugged, but technically backward, so for its post-war project the company hired Palmer, to give them valuable new ideas. Designed while the Second World War was still blazing, the Javelin made its debut in the austerity years which followed, and immediately drew praise because of its style and performance.

By Jowett standards, there was innovation everywhere, not only in the style and the engine, but in the body construction and the use of independent front suspension. Based around a unit-construction four-door saloon body shell, which was supplied by Briggs Motor Bodies in Doncaster, the new Javelin had a high nose but a long sweeping tail, which by the standards of the day was remarkably wind-cheating. Creditable in any other make of car, by Jowett's previous standards it was breathtakingly novel.

The flat-four engine was completely new, and once a series of teething problems had been sorted out, it also proved to be remarkably tuneable. This ensured that Palmer could endow it with sparkling performance – it was at least 10 mph faster than other comparable British 1.5-litre cars of the day – and very capable roadholding. The Javelin soon began to get a name for itself, especially in long-distance rallies, and the arrival of a specialised sports car (the Jupiter) based on the same running gear all helped transform Jowett's reputation. Successful Javelin outings in the French Alpine and Monte Carlo rallies, and by the Jupiter in the Le Mans 24 Hour race, all confirmed the pedigree.

Unfortunately Jowett did not have a vast dealer network with which to tackle their bigger rivals (Ford, Austin and Morris) head on, nor could they sell the Javelin cheaply enough to seriously threaten them, so it was never financially possible to facelift the original style, nor to invest in a new one. Well known transmission reliability problems didn't help; a high selling price also took its toll, and by the early 1950s the Javelin was well past its peak. Even though a new generation Jupiter sports car was being designed, the last cars were built in 1953.

In seven years a total of 22,799 Javelins, and 899 Jupiters, were produced.

Below: The style of the car drew praise with its high nose and long sweeping tail. It had good roadholding and its performance was at least 10 mph faster than other comparable cars of the day.

Jowett Javelin

Years in production: 1947–53
Structure: Front engine/rear-drive. Monocoque body/chassis
Engine type: Flat-four, overhead-valve
Bore and stroke: 72.5 x 90 mm
Capacity: 1,486 cc
Power: 50 bhp @ 4,100 rpm
Fuel supply: Two downdraught Zenith carburettors
Suspension: Independent front, beam-axle rear
Weight: 2,156 lb
Top speed: 78 mph

1948 Jaguar XK120

The XK120 caused a sensation when launched in 1948, and it still turns heads today. Not only was it beautiful, but it was also very fast, had a new type of twin overhead camshaft engine, and was always sold at unbelievably low prices. Yet it had all been developed in a tearing hurry, and was never meant to sell in large numbers.

Jaguar (once known as SS-Jaguar) had started planning for its post-war existence while the bombs were still falling on Coventry. The centre of its strategy was to be the production of new twin-cam engines, which would power a big new saloon car. The problem for Jaguar's founder, William Lyons, was that the engine was ready long before the new car could be finalised. In frustration, therefore, Lyons decided on a short-term solution. After instructing his design team to produce a short-wheelbase version of the new torsion-bar chassis (with a 102 in/2,591 mm wheelbase instead of the original 120 in/3,048 mm), to use the intended engine, transmission and suspension, he personally set about styling a sleek open two-seater sports car body style.

Even though it was revealed in October 1948, the XK120 was not ready for sale until mid 1949. Early cars had wooden body framing clad in aluminium panels, but by 1950–51 this had all changed, and a series production steel body shell of the same shape had taken over. By 1954, when the XK120 gave way to the similar XK140, the open car had been joined by a bubble-top coupé, and by a more fully-equipped drop-head coupé.

The 3.4-litre twin-cam engine was one of the most powerful in the world, ensuring that every XK120 could top 120 mph. Not only that, but it was one of the silkiest and most refined engines Jaguar had produced, the car being equally happy to potter along at 30 mph in towns, or at a stress-free 100 mph on open roads. The engine was so outstanding that it later powered the C-types and D-types which won at Le Mans in the 1950s.

These days we would criticise the XK120's lacklustre drum brakes and the heavy steering, but no-one ever whinged about the acceleration, the style, or the sheer animal character which was built in to every car. Not only was the XK120 wildly successful all over the world, but it was also a great rally car, and in some events a useful race car too. In six years, 12,055 cars were produced.

To replace it, Jaguar would need an excellent car. Fortunately the XK140, based on the same design but with more power, and most of the drawbacks eliminated, was just that. The XK pedigree continued until 1961 when the first of the equally amazing E-types appeared, while the last of the XK engines was not built until the 1990s.

Jaguar XK120

Years in production: 1949–54
Structure: Front engine/rear-drive. Separate chassis
Engine type: 6-cylinder, twin-over head-camshaft
Bore and stroke: 83 x 106 mm
Capacity: 3,442 cc
Power: 160 bhp @ 5,000 rpm
Fuel supply: Two horizontal SU carburettors
Suspension: Independent front, beam-axle rear
Weight: 2,856 lb
Top speed: 125 mph

Left and below: This car caused a sensation when it was launched. It was very successful worldwide and a great rally car.

1948 Land Rover

Here is a classic case of the stop-gap project which soon outgrew its parent. Before the Land Rover appeared, Rover had been building a relatively small number of fine middle class cars. By the 1950s they were building many more Land Rover 4x4s, and the cars were very much a minor part of the business.

Immediately after the war, Rover found itself running a massive former 'shadow factory' complex at Solihull, and needed to fill it. (A 'shadow factory' was an aero-engine factory established during the rearmament of the 1930s.) Faced with material shortages, it could not build many private cars, and elected to fill the gaps with a newly-developed 4x4, which it would base unashamedly on the design of the already legendary Jeep from the USA.

Early Land Rovers shared the same 80 in/2,032 mm wheelbase as the Jeep, and the same basic four-wheel-drive layout. The Land Rover, however, was much more versatile than the Jeep, in that it was built in myriad different guises, shapes and derivatives, and it used aluminium body panels, which ensured that it was virtually rust-free. Apart from the fact that it was not very fast or powerful, (though time and further development would solve those problems) the Land Rover could tackle almost any job, climb almost any slope, and ford almost every stream, which made it invaluable for farmers, contractors, surveyors, explorers, armies, public service companies – in fact almost anyone with a need for four-wheel-drive traction, and the rugged construction which went with it.

It wasn't long before the original pick-up was joined by vans, estate cars, short and long wheelbases to choice, petrol and diesel engines. A long list of extras became available: winches, extra-large wheels and tyres, and liaison with specialist companies ensured that it could be turned it into an impromptu railway shunting vehicle, a portable cinema truck, an equipment hoist, and a whole lot more. Its short-travel leaf spring suspension gave it a shatteringly hard ride and the Land Rover engineers stated that this, at least, limited cross-country speeds to keep the chassis in one piece.

Later models grew larger, longer, and more powerful, but it would not be until the 1960s that the first six-cylinder type appeared, not until 1979 that the first V8 Land Rover was sold, and not until the early 1980s that coil spring suspension finally took over. Sales, however, just went on and on, with the millionth being produced in the mid 1970s. By the late 1990s, when the 'Freelander' model appeared, 1.5 million Land Rovers had been manufactured, although by then it had been renamed 'Defender' and was sold exclusively with diesel engines.

Right: Based on the American Jeep car, this British 4x4 used aluminium panels to produce a virtually rust-free vehicle in a variety of shapes and styles.

Land Rover

Years in production:	(Series I) 1948–57
Structure:	Front engine/four-wheel-drive. Separate chassis
Engine type:	4-cylinder, overhead-inlet-valve/side exhaust
Bore and stroke:	69.5 x 105 mm
Capacity:	1,595 cc
Power:	50 bhp @ 4,000 rpm
Fuel supply:	One downdraught Solex carburettor
Suspension:	Beam-axle front, beam-axle rear
Weight:	2,594 lb
Top speed:	55 mph

1948 Morris Minor

The Morris Minor, like the Mini, is one of those cars that everyone recalls, affectionately, with a nostalgic smile. 'Ah, yes,' we all say, 'I used to have one of those when I was young....' Morris Minors are now seen as fully paid-up classic cars, not for their performance, nor for their style, but for their unmistakable character. Then, as now, no-one drives a Morris Minor if they are in a hurry, for although the roadholding was peerless by late 1940s standards, the acceleration was distinctly leisurely.

It all started in 1942-43, when Morris Motors' Alec Issigonis first sketched out his ideas for a new post-war small car. Egged on by the vice-chairman, Miles Thomas, his small team designed the 'Mosquito' around a squat unit-construction body shell, which was to be powered by a new type of flat-four cylinder engine. Post-war shortages and a lack of capital caused delays, the new engine was swept away in favour of an ancient side-valve unit, and the entire shell was widened at the last minute, but the Morris Minor which went on sale in 1948 was still an intriguing proposition. At a time when most British cars looked narrow and old-fashioned, the new-shape Minor was arresting, had torsion bar front suspension to provide great handling, and rack-and-pinion steering to provide precise direction.

The fact that the top speed was little more than 60 mph, and that the styling was not to everyone's taste (Lord Nuffield himself is supposed to have likened it to 'a bloody poached egg') made no difference. For the next two decades Nuffield (and later BMC) sold Minors just as fast as they could be made.

Here was a range that grew and grew. Over the years saloons, open-top tourers, estate cars, vans and pick-ups were all eventually made in large numbers; the floor pan and suspension was adapted for use under the Wolseley 1500/Riley 1.5-litre models, while the cars were assembled locally in several parts of the Commonwealth.

Morris Minor

Years in production: 1948–71
Structure: Front engine/rear-drive. Monocoque body/chassis
ORIGINAL TYPE:
Engine type: 4-cylinder, side-valve.
Bore and stroke: 57 x 90 mm
Capacity: 917 cc
Power: 27 bhp @ 4,000 rpm
Fuel supply: One horizontal SU carburettor
Suspension: Independent front, beam-axle rear
Weight: 1,735 lb
Top speed: 62 mph

From 1952 Series II Minors got a new overhead-valve engine, but no more performance, and from 1956 they became Morris Minor 1000s, with a more powerful 948 cc engine. The last Minors of all had 1.1-litre engines, but by that time they had become institutions, and no-one really measured the performance.

Minor styling changed little over the years, although the headlamp position was raised in the early 1950s, and bow windows front and rear) were part of the Minor 1000 package of 1956. The splendid

roadholding, the rather boomy exhaust note, and the way it acquired and kept its 'district nurse's car' image all remained constant.

The sales figures tell their own story, for in 21 years, 1948–71, no fewer than 1.3 million Minors (and another quarter-million vans and pick-ups) were sold. In later years some were also made in Sri Lanka, and it is still possible to recreate a Morris Minor today.

To some people, there has never been a more practical car.

Above and right: These are cars which evoke nostalgia as their character is what made them so popular. Produced in a wide range of styles, the cars were to become an institution and they never lost their 'district nurse's car' image.

1948 Bond Minicar 3-wheeler

Cars like the Bond could only have prospered in a motoring climate which was starved of both cars and fuel – which explains why these ingeniously-detailed three-wheelers were so successful in the 1940s and 1950s. Over the years, several generations were produced around the same basic structure, where the engine was mounted close to the single front wheel, driving and steering with it; reverse gear was not offered.

Lawrie Bond, sometimes described as an eccentric genius, designed the original car before selling the manufacturing rights to Sharps Commercials of Preston, Lancashire, who were soon building 15 cars every week. The Minicar's secret was its tiny, two-seater size, its light but amazingly effective aluminium structure (there was no separate chassis), and for the way the air-cooled single-cylinder motor cycle-type engine was arranged to drive the single front wheel by chain, and to pivot with that wheel when it was turned to steer the car.

Crude in almost every other way, it was nevertheless an amazingly compact little car: the original models had no rear suspension, (the rear wheels' only function was to keep the rear end of the car off the ground), 30 mph was really the limit of the cruising speed, and creature comforts were in line with the low price. Lacking a reverse gear, it could be driven by anyone possessing a motor cycle licence, though because the front wheel could be steered to a full 90 degrees in each direction on later cars, the lack of that reverse was no big loss; the Minicar, quite literally, could turn in its own length.

Yet, for all this, the original Minicar cost only £199 (half the price of a Morris Minor), there was a serviceable hood and removable side screens, the cars often returned an amazing 100 mpg on two-stroke fuel, and they would not, of course, rust. To drive and enjoy a Bond, however, needed a certain attitude of mind, for all journeys tended to be slow, long and tedious, the driver always felt vulnerable when surrounded by other traffic, and if social status mattered to him, he was advised to choose another mode of transport.

Many ex-motorcyclists, and marginal motorists, shrugged off all this, and a whole series of Minicars, which became progressively larger, more streamlined, and more expensive, followed, until the last was produced in 1966. By then Sharps had turned to producing the Bond Equipe sports coupé, a much more upmarket machine – yet 26,500 Minicar sales, in 18 years, told its own success story. In spite of their rust-resistant construction, very few seem to have survived.

Bond Minicar 3-wheeler

Years in production: 1948–51
Structure: Front engine/front-wheel-drive. Aluminium monocoque body/chassis
Engine type: 1-cylinder, two-stroke
Capacity: 122 cc
Power: 5 bhp @ 4,400 rpm
Fuel supply: One horizontal Amal carburettor
Suspension: Independent front, Solid/no suspension rear
Weight: 308 lb
Top speed: 35 mph

Left and below: These three-wheelers were very successful due to their tiny size and their rust-free aluminium structure. They had no reverse gear and could be driven by anyone with a motorcycle licence.

1949 Healey Silverstone

Although everyone now remembers Donald Healey for the famous Austin-Healey sports cars which bear his name, his reputation was secure well before then. Triumph's technical chief in the 1930s, he established his own sports car business immediately after the Second World War, and a whole family of sports saloons, drop-head coupés and two-seaters evolved around the same chassis. The Silverstone, of which only 105 cars were ever made, was the most sporty of all.

The chassis was a simple, but rigid, box-section design, with a 102 in (2591 mm) wheelbase, which featured trailing-arm/coil spring independent front suspension. Although originally intended to use Triumph running gear, (Healey tried to sell the rights to his one-time employer), it was finally powered by the impressive twin high-camshaft Riley 2.5-litre engine, whose 104 bhp output was among the highest of all early post-war British cars. Backed by a Riley gearbox and rear axle, this was a formidable base on which to build various body styles.

Original cars, pre-viewed in 1946, were two-door four-seater machines called Westland (an open roadster) and Elliot (a saloon), but although both could reach 100 mph, they were really too heavy to be competitive in motorsport. The two-seater Silverstone, which was announced in 1949, changed all that.

Using the same chassis, the Silverstone was fitted with a stark and very basically equipped open-top aluminium body shell in a traditional two-seater style. With separate front wings closely cowling the front wheels, the head-lamps were hidden away behind a narrow radiator grille – where they can have done little to improve the air flow through the radiator. The Silverstone was 450 to 500 lb (204 to 227 kg) lighter than the four-seater types, and the trade-off for minimal accommodation was much faster acceleration, and better roadholding. One of the entertaining quirks of this car, by the way, was that the spare wheel was mounted horizontally, and semi-externally in the tail, where it acted as a bumper. There was no front bumper.

Functionally, this was a purposeful machine, the only marketing problem being that it was handbuilt and, by definition, expensive. Unhappily, some potential customers wanted a fast car as an alternative to, say, the Jaguar XK120, but were frightened off the Silverstone because it was such an individual machine. It might have been effective, but as there was virtually nowhere to stow any luggage, here was a single-purpose car, made with motorsport in mind.

Only 105 Silverstones were made, and all today's survivors are regarded as rare, and desirable machines.

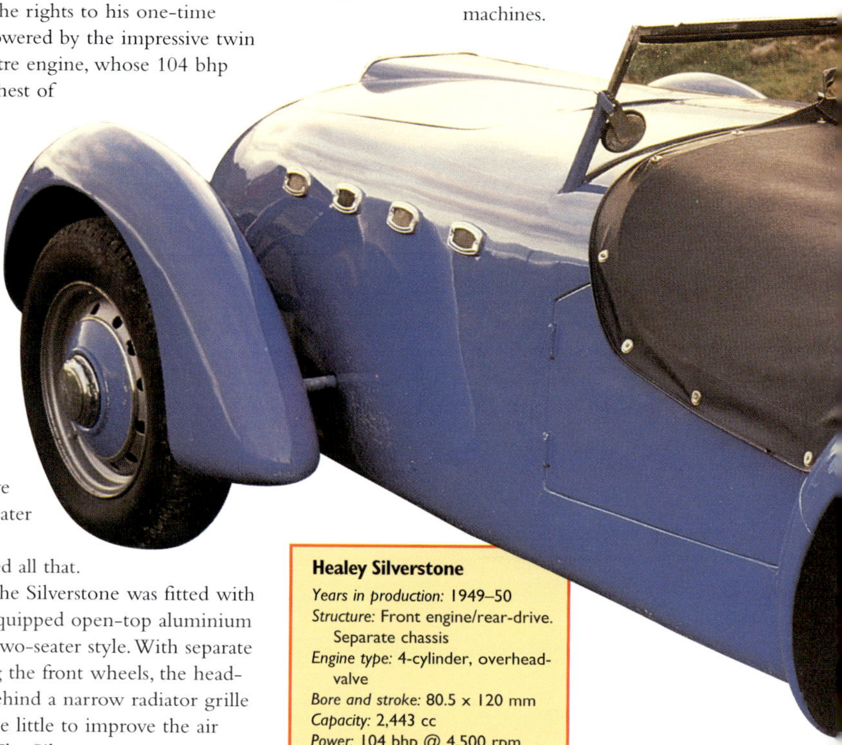

Healey Silverstone

Years in production: 1949–50
Structure: Front engine/rear-drive. Separate chassis
Engine type: 4-cylinder, overhead-valve
Bore and stroke: 80.5 x 120 mm
Capacity: 2,443 cc
Power: 104 bhp @ 4,500 rpm
Fuel supply: Two horizontal SU carburettors
Suspension: Independent front, beam-axle rear
Weight: 2,072 lb
Top speed: 105 mph

Below and right: Made of aluminium, these cars had their headlamps hidden away behind the radiator grille. The spare wheel was mounted horizontally, and semi-externally in the tail, where it acted as a bumper. Handbuilt, these were expensive cars and survivors are very rare.

1949 Dellow Sports Car

With great shortage of new cars after the Second World War, almost any product calling itself a sports car found a market. The Dellow, which was produced by a small garage business near Birmingham, was one such. Its instigators, K.C. Delingpole and Ron Lowe, were production car trials enthusiasts, so they produced a car which could be used as both a two-seater sports car on the road and as a trials car.

Built around a simple tubular chassis frame, it used mainly Ford Ten/Prefect components, including the rugged 1,172 cc side-valve engine and a three-speed gearbox, with the old-fashioned transverse leaf suspension. The original cars were bodied in stark two-seater open-top style, using aluminium skin panels on a tubular frame work. Naturally, there were no doors, a skimpy soft-top was only provided as an apology for keeping out the worst of the bad weather, while two trials-orientated features were the big (15 gallon) fuel tank, and the twin spare wheels, both of which hung out over the rear of the car, thus increasing the weight over the driven rear wheels.

The result was a perky, quirky, but above all light, cheap and appealing little two-seater, which soon built up its own small coterie of fans. Eventually outclassed in trials, where more specialised machinery eventually took over, the Dellow was also a good car for use in driving tests and some rallies.

Compared with almost any other British car of the day – and certainly any family car – the original Dellow was outrageously stark and purposeful. Even though the side-valve-engined Fords were nothing special, and the three-speed gearbox was a positive drawback, this car was so light that it was brisk and appealing. Even in standard form they could reach 70 mph, but when super-tuned, speeds of 80 mph (which felt and sounded most impressive) were seen.

Later Dellows had coil spring suspension on their beam-axles, but by the mid-1950s their time had passed. No more than 500 cars of all types were ever made.

Dellow Sports Car

Years in production: 1949–57
Structure: Front engine/ rear-drive. Separate chassis
Engine type: 4-cylinder, side-valve
Bore and stroke: 63.5 x 92.5 mm
Capacity: 1,172 cc
Power: 30 bhp @ 4,000 rpm
Fuel supply: One down-draught Zenith carburettor
Suspension: Beam-axle front, beam-axle rear
Weight: 1,344 lb
Top speed: 69 mph

Above: This open-topped two-seater, was a car with no opening doors and aluminium skin panels. The cars were light, cheap and appealing with two spare tyres mounted on the rear of the car.

1949 Rover P4

If ever there was a model which deserved the famous nickname of 'Auntie Rover', this was it. The legendary P4 saloon, first seen in 1949, but gradually developed, was the epitome of everything Rover's guiding light, Spencer Wilks, was trying to do. High performance meant nothing to him, but refinement, high quality and dignity was of utmost importance. At this time Rover's measured, gradual but totally focused approach to building, equipping and marketing its cars had been maturing for well over a decade, for it was the arrival of Wilks as Rover's managing director in the 1930s which had made it all possible.

The P4 (which indicated that this was the first phase in a long-term plan of model development) was much like its predecessors, though it looked more modern and incorporated a number of mechanical innovations. Based around a four-door saloon style on a rock-solid separate chassis, the car's original engine was a 2.2-litre 75 bhp straight-six, and the '75' set about providing motoring for the 'mobile drawing room' class.

This was not a car in which one set out to drive fast; instead one motored in great comfort, safety and with pleasure. It was quiet, it felt quite insulated from the world outside, and it never seemed to be in a hurry. The P4 had all the old-fashioned virtues of grace, understated good taste, long experience, and a certain standing in society, so it was no wonder that, quite without Rover's intention, it soon became known as 'Auntie Rover'. In the same way that many people's favourite aunt might be well dressed and immaculately turned out, so a P4 was impressively equipped, the inside having wood, leather and pile carpets in abundance.

Rover had invested heavily in the P4; it intended to sell it for a long time, gradually making logical changes and improvements. The only startling feature of the original shape was the central 'Cyclops' lamp in the grille, but this disappeared in the first facelift, while later alterations squared up the rear of the body a little, and increased the size of the rear window.

Over the years, therefore, the main changes were to the engines and the transmission. Using the model name to indicate peak power output, the six-cylinder unit was eventually enlarged and pushed out through '90', '95', '100' and finally '110' (the fastest of these cars could reach 100 mph), while at one time there were also four-cylinder '60' and '80' varieties. All these, and the choice of freewheel, overdrive or automatic transmissions meant that there was plenty for the customers to choose from.

A typical P4 customer, by the way, might be a doctor, a solicitor, a bank manager or an accountant, but one rarely found sporting types such as racing drivers or young tycoons signing an order form. According to Rover, this was exactly as it should be, and before the P4 was finally displaced by the very different P6 2000 in 1964, more than 130,000 cars had been built.

Rover P4

Years in production: 1949–64, all models
Structure: Front engine/rear-drive. Separate chassis
ORIGINAL 75 MODEL
Engine type: 6-cylinder, overhead inlet/side-exhaust-valve
Bore and stroke: 65.2 x 105 mm
Capacity: 2,103 cc
Power: 75 bhp @ 4,200 rpm
Fuel supply: Two horizontal SU carburettors
Suspension: Independent front, beam-axle rear
Weight: 3,265 lb
Top speed: 82 mph

Above: This high quality, four-door saloon was well-equipped with wood, leather and pile carpets. Built for comfort, safety and pleasure, this was not a fast car.

S 810

1950 Ford Consul/Zephyr Six

Until the 1950s, British Fords were always affectionately known as 'Dagenham Dustbins' (cars were built at Dagenham, in Essex), with their engineering derided, and their low selling prices highly respected. All that changed forever when the first post-war Fords were introduced. The closely related Consul and Zephyr models completely changed the face of the company.

After 1945 it took several years to convert the British motor industry to a forward-looking peacetime economy. Even at Ford, a ruthlessly efficient operation, early post-war cars were simply warmed-over 1930s types until the introduction of the Consul/Zephyr models, classics of their type, and classic to this day. Inside Ford, and out, these cars represented a design revolution. They were the first Fords to use unit construction (chassis-less), the first to use independent front suspension, and the first to use overhead valve engines. Later, as the model range developed, they would be the first to offer a steel-bodied estate car derivative, the first to offer automatic transmission as an option, and the first Fords to go on sale with front-wheel-disc brakes.

Even if they had looked dreadful, they would have been classics of their period, but this excuse was never needed. Styled by Ford-USA in Detroit, they were modern, streamlined, distinctive shapes by the standards of the late 1940s. Inside their cabins, of course, they were pure Detroit, complete with bench-type front seats, and with steering-column gear change controls.

Under the skin, Consuls had four-cylinder and Zephyrs had six-cylinder versions of the same design, while the front suspension was a new and mechanically simple layout known as 'MacPherson strut' (after its American inventor) which was carefully patented to eliminate direct copies. The mechanical elegance of this system was such, however, that rivals all round the world made haste to make their own versions (and to employ the best patent lawyers to advise them).

Consuls had a soft ride, but were quite slow, while

Ford Consul / Zephyr Six

Years in production: 1950–1956
Structure: Front engine/ rear-drive. Monocoque body/chassis
Engine type: 4-cylinder/ 6-cylinder, overhead-valve
Bore and stroke: 79.37 x 76.2 mm
Capacity: 1,508 cc/2,262 cc
Power: 47 bhp @ 4,400 rpm/68 bhp @ 4,000 rpm
Fuel supply: One downdraught Zenith carburettor
Suspension: Independent front, beam-axle rear
Weight: 2,296 lb/2,604 lb
Top speed: 74 mph/80 mph

Zephyrs (which had a longer wheelbase) were faster, but with rather skittish roadholding. Their value, however, was not in doubt, and after a 'works' Zephyr had won the Monte Carlo Rally in 1953, their reputation was sealed.

Shortly, a better-trimmed and equipped version of the Zephyr, called 'Zodiac', arrived, after which developments of these cars dominated their market sector for more than 20 years, until the first Granadas replaced them. As model followed model, rivals would snipe about their styling, their equipment, and their rather obvious transatlantic pedigree, but Ford, who knew what sort of value they were offering, never flinched.

Between 1950 and 1956, no fewer than 231,481 Consul/Zephyrs were sold.

Above: This was an innovative car from Ford. Their style was distinctive, modern and streamlined. They were styled by Ford-USA and had bench front seats and steering-column gear change controls.

1950 MG TD

If ever there was a car which introduced American drivers to the British sports car, it was the MG TD. Earlier T-Series cars had reached the USA in limited numbers, but it was the TD – the first MG sports car to have a left-hand-drive option, and the first to have independent front suspension – that converted them. Of a total production of nearly 30,000, more than 23,000 were originally sold in North America.

Building on the reputation of its earlier Midgets, MG had launched the first T-Series car in 1936, but until 1950 they had a 1930s layout, complete with a flexible chassis, a narrow-hipped body and a bone-shattering ride. The TD, which was developed in a tearing hurry, set out to change all that.

Although the TD followed the same visual philosophy as previous Midgets – a wooden-framed body tub, flowing front wings, separate free-standing headlamps, and an upright, instantly recognisable radiator grille – it was different in almost every detail. Not only had the chassis, hidden underneath, been changed, but the proportions of the body shell had altered too.

The first prototype used a much-changed version of the MG YA chassis, but for production there was a new frame, much stiffer than ever before, with wider wheel tracks, rack-and-pinion steering and coil spring independent front suspension. Although the engine and transmission similar to the TC Midget which it replaced, the TD turned out to be a much more capable car, if only because its roadholding was so much better than before.

This was, in other words, a new type of sports car which, quite perversely, continued to look old. Except that it was wider and somewhat more squat than before, it could easily have been engineered in the 1930s, and was built on the same sort of rudimentary jigging and tooling. For a time, at least, absolutely no-one complained, especially when they discovered the famous XPAG-type engine which could withstand super-tuning, and realised that the car could develop spirited acceleration. Nothing, however, could give the TD a high top speed, as its body had all the aerodynamic qualities of a mature barn door.

Until two new and much more modern looking sports cars appeared – the Triumph TR2 and the Austin-Healey 100 – the TD was Britain's most successful sports car, and deservedly so. It was probably a mistake for MG's bosses to insist that it was than facelifted (to the TF) instead of commissioning a completely new style, but these cars won, and have always retained, a huge following, especially now that the cult of the classic car has mushroomed so strongly.

MG TD

Years in production: 1949–53
Structure: Front engine/rear-drive. Separate chassis
Engine type: 4-cylinder, overhead-valve
Bore and stroke: 66.5 x 90 mm
Capacity: 1,250 cc
Power: 54 bhp @ 5,200 rpm
Fuel supply: Two horizontal SU
Suspension: Independent front, beam-axle rear
Weight: 1,930 lb
Top speed: 77 mph

Right: The TD differed from previous Midgets in its chassis and body shell. These cars had much better roadholding than earlier models and went on to become Britain's most successful sports car.

KWS 101

1951 Standard Vanguard

Standard's original post-war Vanguard may not be classic in terms of its performance or roadholding, but it was in terms of what it set out to do. Immediately after the Second World War, Britain's car makers were exhorted to adopt one-model policies, and for a time this was Standard's response.

The government's 'one-size-fits-all' policy was never going to produce thoroughbreds, but with exports to the Empire in mind, and by designing a new engine which was ideal for use in the Ferguson tractor, Standard produced an ordinary but remarkably rugged machine. In a clever and patriotic move they chose to name it 'Vanguard', after Britain's only surviving modern battleship.

Although the rather short-wheelbase chassis layout was very ordinary, and the original body style rather too obviously derived from transatlantic trends, its origins were fascinating. Concluding that early 1940s Plymouths were among the most attractive of American shapes, Standard's managing director had sent his chief stylist down to London, to sit outside the American embassy, and to sketch any Plymouth he found parked outside.

The engine was a heavy four-cylinder affair, with slip-fit 'wet' cylinder liners. Inspired by the current front-wheel-drive Citroen power unit, it would survive for more than 20 years, to power Vanguards and Ferguson tractors, as well as a long line of fast, reliable and successful Triumph TR sports cars.

Purists did not like the style, the use of bench front seats, the three-speed gearboxes or the steering column gear change, but export customers clearly did, especially as they soon found that the Vanguard could put up with rough treatment, misuse and neglect on a grand scale. Vanguards were soon found not only in London, but in Cape Town, Sydney and North America. The armed forces bought them in large numbers, and to keep up with the demand Standard also made them available in saloon, estate, van or pick-up form ('ute', to use the Australian phrase, where these versions were built).

Although bodies tended to go rusty (but what post-war British car did not, because of poor quality steel being supplied?), the rest of the running seemed to last forever, so many of these cars still survive. The original car was re-styled, into the notchback Vanguard Phase II, in 1953, then an entirely different type of car, the monocoque chassised Mk III, followed in 1955. The theme changed completely in the mid 1960s, when a much better car, the Triumph 2000 took over.

Right: Heavily based on the American Plymouths, these cars were soon very popular all over the world. They were produced in saloon, estate, van or pick-up form and many cars still survive.

Standard Vanguard
Years in production: 1948–53
Structure: Front engine/rear-drive. Separate chassis
Engine type: 4-cylinder, overhead-valve
Bore and stroke: 85 x 92 mm
Capacity: 2,088 cc
Power: 68 bhp @ 4,200 rpm
Fuel supply: One downdraught Solex carburettor
Suspension: Independent front, beam-axle rear
Weight: 2,620 lb
Top speed: 78 mph

Standard

1952 Bentley Continental R-Type

After Rolls-Royce took over Bentley in 1931, it was more than 20 years before the new owners produced another truly sporty new model. But the wait was worthwhile. The R-type Continental of 1952–55 was a great car by any standards, which not only looked sensational, but was also extremely fast.

Even before 1939, Rolls-Royce had dabbled with super-streamlined prototypes (one of them being called a 'Bentley Corniche'), but production cars had to wait until after the war. Using only slightly modified versions of the existing Bentley Mk VI saloon car's chassis, but with a superbly detailed two-door four-seater coupé designed by the coachbuilder, H.J. Mulliner, the company produced an extremely fast (115 mph), exclusive, and very expensive car, whose title told its own story.

The Continental certainly did not gain its high performance by being light, but by a combination of high (unstated) horsepower, and by the remarkable aerodynamic performance of the bulky, yet sleek shell. There was, of course, no way of taming the drag of the proud Bentley radiator grille, but the lines of the rest of the car were as wind-cheating as possible, the long tapering tail being a delight to the eyes. Like all the best 1930s Bentleys, it had two passenger doors, and a full four-seater package. Leather, carpet and wood abounded – for no concessions were made to ensure a high performance.

Bentley Continental R-type
Years in production: 1952–1955
Structure: Front engine/rear-drive. Separate chassis
Engine type: 6-cylinder, overhead-valve inlet/side exhaust
Bore and stroke: 92.1 x 114.3 mm/ 95.25 x 114.3 mm
Capacity: 4,566/4,887 cc
Power: Not revealed
Fuel supply: Two horizontal SU carburettors
Suspension: Independent front, beam-axle rear
Weight: 3,700 lb
Top speed: 115/118 mph

Here was an expensive grand tourer for the connoisseur and, by definition, it was likely to sell in small numbers. Put on sale in 1952 at £7,608 (at a time when Morris Minor prices, for instance, started at £582), it was ideal for the 'sportsman' who liked to drive far and fast, wherever conditions allowed. It was produced in the traditional Bentley/Rolls-Royce style, for the engine was low-revving, the steering and most other controls quite heavy, and the fuel consumption ferocious – but the fit, finish and quality of every component (especially the interior trim) were of the very highest quality.

As ever, Rolls-Royce/Bentley never thought it necessary to reveal the power output of the big six-cylinder engine, whose overhead inlet/side exhaust valve layout was only shared with one other British make of car – the Rover of the period. Needing only to point out the easily provable performance of their cars, they let acceleration figures speak for themselves.

In a career of only three years, the R-type Continental needed little improvement, for the engine was a very powerful 4.5-litre unit. Only 208 were ever built.

Above and below: A great sporty new model which looked sensational and performed very well. They had a long tapering tail and leather, wood and carpet built into the interior design which was of the highest quality.

1953 Triumph TR2

Although Triumph was originally an independent car-maker, it was taken over by Standard in 1944. Several early post-war attempts to sell 'Standard-Triumphs' all failed, but after Standard also failed to take over Morgan, Sir John Black told his engineers to develop a rival sports car.

Work on the 20TS project began in 1952, the prototype being shown at Earls Court in October of that year. A very tight budget obliged the engineers to base the original design around a modified 1930s-style Standard Flying Nine frame, which was clearly not stiff enough. That first car was neither fast enough, nor attractive enough, and lacked proper road behaviour.

A rapid and complete re-design produced the definitive TR2 of 1953, which had a new and more rigid chassis frame, coil spring independent front suspension, a 90 bhp development of the Standard Vanguard engine, modified and more chunky rear-end styling, and a top speed of more than 100 mph. The first production cars were delivered in the autumn of 1953 at the bargain price of £787, and were immediately seen as serious competition for MG, whose old-fashioned TF's top speed was 20 mph slower.

Although the TR2 was fast and remarkably cheap, its handling was still somewhat suspect, and it was fortunate that an outright win in the 1954 RAC Rally of March 1954 brought an instant competition record to the notice of motoring enthusiasts. Sales rose gradually (especially in North America) as the car improved, and as the available extras (including a removable hard-top, wire-spoke wheels, and overdrive) proliferated. The remarkable fact which also began to emerge from countless magazine road tests was that a TR2 could not only be a race and a rally winner, it could also be extremely economical: 32-35 mpg was normal for the early cars.

In the autumn of 1955, only two years after the first TR2 had been delivered, it was replaced by the TR3, which had minor styling changes, and 95 bhp. In the next year the engine power crept up again – to 100 bhp – and from late 1956 the TR3 became the world's first quantity-production sports car to have front-wheel disc brakes as standard.

More improvements followed. From the autumn of 1957 (for launch in January 1958) the car was built

with revised front-end styling and other equipment improvements. Soon affectionately known as the TR3A, this was a title never officially adopted by the Triumph concern. It was the TR3A which really found great popularity in North America, where most sales were made, and which established the marque's fine reputation in that continent in advance of the introduction of Spitfires and newer TRs in the 1960s.

A 2,138 cc engine became optional in 1959, after it had been used successfully in the 1958 Alpine Rally by the factory team, though few cars with this engine appear to have been sold. TR3A production continued until 1961, when the model was replaced by the TR4, which had a completely new body shell. A final series of cars was built in 1962 to satisfy Triumph's North American dealers. Unofficially known as TR3Bs, and only for sale in the USA, most had 2,138 cc engines, and all used the TR4-type synchromesh gearbox.

There were 8,628 TR2s, 13,377 TR3s and 58,236 TR3As, along with 3,331 TR3Bs. The vast majority of these cars were exported, most of them to the USA.

Triumph TR2

Years in production: (TR2–TR3B) 1953–1962
Structure: Front engine/rear-drive. Separate chassis
Engine type: Four-cylinder, overhead-valve
Bore and stroke: 83 x 92 mm
Capacity: 1,991 cc
Power: 90 bhp @ 4,800 rpm
Fuel supply: Two horizontal SU carburettors
Suspension: Independent front, beam-axle rear
Weight: 1,848 lb
Top speed: 103 mph

Above and below: This was a car which was seen as serious competition for the MG. It could be both an economical road car and a race and rally winner.

1955 MG MGA

In the 1930s and 1940s, MG established a world-wide reputation for producing small, neat, two-seater sports cars with lots of character. By the 1950s, however, the traditional styles on which they had concentrated were beginning to look dated, so MG enthusiasts were delighted when the all-new MGA was announced in 1955.

Compared with the long-running T-series cars, which it replaced at Abingdon, the MGA was different in every respect. Not only did it have a new, broad-based chassis frame, and a modern and very stylish body, but it was the first MG sports car to use BMC (Austin-based), instead of Nuffield-based running gear. All previous MGs had used engines derived from Morris and Wolseley family cars, while the MGA used engines which had been designed for use in new BMC family cars.

Inspiration for the MGA originally came from a special body which MG built for a T-series model to race at Le Mans in 1951. It was refined and made more 'production' over the next four years. Smooth where previous MGs had been craggy, wide where they had been narrow, and roomy where they had been cramped, it was an elegant leap into the future.

Sitting on a new, squat and very sturdy chassis frame, the new MGA body was the first all-new MG styling since the arrival of the Midgets in the 1930s. Built entirely from steel pressings (though wooden floor boards were retained), it married a sloping version of the familiar MG grille with a flowing, sexy, shape.

The engine was a tuned-up BMC B-series, previously used in the MG Magnette sports saloon, and although traditionalists complained about this at first, it proved to be just as tuneable as any previous MG power unit. Even when rated at 72 bhp, it gave the MGA a top speed approaching 100 mph, while up to 100 bhp was available in racing form.

The MGA not only looked beautiful, but also had a

MG MGA

Years in production: (All types) 1955–62
Structure: Front engine/rear-drive. Separate chassis
Engine type: 4-cylinder, overhead-valve
ORIGINAL 1500:
Bore and stroke: 73.02 x 88.9 mm
Capacity: 1,489 cc
Power: 72 bhp @ 5,500 rpm
Fuel supply: Two horizontal SU carburettors
Suspension: Independent front, beam-axle rear
Weight: 1,988 lb
Top speed: 98 mph

soft ride, very good roadholding, and seemed to be stuffed full of 'Abingdon magic'. It immediately began to outsell any previous MG car, and when a neat bubble-top coupé, with wind-up windows, was added, the range was complete.

Over the years the MGA was progressively improved: the 1600 of 1959 had a larger engine and front disc brakes, and finally the Mk II of 1961, which had 86 bhp and a 101 mph top speed. For a time, too, there was even an expensive, difficult-to-maintain MGA twin-cam, with a unique engine. A great car was needed to improve on the MGA, and the MGB was just that. In seven years, no fewer than 101,470 MGAs were built, then an Abingdon record.

Above: A beautiful car with good roadholding and a soft ride. They were the first MGs to use BMC engines as opposed to the Morris and Wolseley in previous models.

1958 Armstrong-Siddeley Star Sapphire

It is ironic that the best and most handsome of all Armstrong-Siddeley saloons was also the last car it ever made. In the UK, the market for large, middle class machines was increasingly dominated by Jaguar, and though the Sapphire and Star Sapphire types had fine engines and attractive styles, they could not compete on price.

Above: The noble radiator shell and emblem.
Right: The elegant cars of Armstrong Siddeley faced strong competition from Jaguar, Alvis and Daimler.

From the 1920s to the 1950s, Armstrong-Siddeley had built a series of well engineered, dignified, but essentially mainstream middle class cars. Then, buoyed up by the profits from their successful aero-engine business, they invested in a new and more advanced range of cars, the Sapphire.

This car had a separate chassis frame and would retain the pre-selector type of transmission for which the marque was noted, but there were two other major innovations. One was that Armstrong-Siddeley elected to assemble their own smart new four-door body shells, and the other was that they designed a new six-cylinder engine, with part-spherical combustion chambers and complex valve gear. The Sapphire of 1953, originally with its 125 bhp/3.4-litre six-cylinder engine, could reach more than 90 mph, and went on sale for £1,728, intending to capture sales in the Jaguar Mk VII market sector. Complete with its noble radiator shell and emblem, and elegant four-door styling, it was a fine machine. With the 150 bhp engine which was also available, it could just reach the magic 100 mph mark.

Right from the start, however, the Sapphire had to face formidable competition, not only from Jaguar, but from Alvis and Daimler. Easier availability, lower prices and a bit more performance would all have helped, but Armstrong-Siddeley's Coventry factory was not capable of mass production, and the Sapphire became rather an exclusive car.

A massive limousine version was soon made available, but it was the much-improved Star Sapphire, built from 1958 to 1960, which was the star of this range. Looking like, but not identical, to the original car, the 'Star' had a 165 bhp/4-litre version of the engine, Borg Warner automatic transmission, power-assisted steering and front wheel disc brakes, in what was a very appealing package.

The price of this most comprehensively equipped car, unhappily, had shot up to £2,646, which was too costly to sustain high sales, and although it was a nicely-built, well equipped and very capable saloon, demand slowly ebbed away. Rootes, in the meantime, had copied the engine for a new Humber Super Snipe, in return for letting Armstrong-Siddeley build Sunbeam Alpine sports cars.

In 1960 Armstrong-Siddeley decided to concentrate on making aircraft engines, and pulled out of the car business completely. Between 1953 and 1960, 8,568 cars in this family were produced.

Armstrong-Siddeley Star Sapphire

Years in production: 1958–60
Structure: Front engine/rear-drive. Separate chassis
Engine type: 6-cylinder, overhead-valve
Bore and stroke: 97 x 90 mm
Capacity: 3,990 cc
Power: 165 bhp @ 4,250 rpm
Fuel supply: Two downdraught Stromberg carburettors
Suspension: Independent front, beam-axle rear
Weight: 3,920 lb
Top speed: 100 mph

1958 Austin-Healey Sprite

Everyone wanted small sports cars in the 1950s, but none were available. Until, that is, BMC asked Donald Healey to design a small two-seater for the Austin-Healey stable. The result was the Sprite, a car which started a new trend. An ever-improving family of Sprites emerged from the MG Abingdon factory until 1971, and the MG Midget which derived from them would be made until 1979.

Spiritually, the new Sprite was related to several earlier BMC cars (MG T-series Midgets because of their size, MGAs and Austin-Healey 100 Sixes) because of the way they also used so many existing parts, such as engines, transmissions and suspension units. Although the car's monocoque structure was new and unique, with a neat way of locating the rear axle by cantilever leaf springs, almost all its running gear was lifted from the BMC 'parts bin', which meant that it would be easy to maintain, and support, at dealerships all over the world.

Austin-Healey Sprite

Years in production: 1958–61
Structure: Front engine/rear-drive. Monocoque body/chassis
Engine type: 4-cylinder, overhead-valve
Bore and stroke: 62.94 x 76.2 mm
Capacity: 948 cc
Power: 43 bhp @ 5,200 rpm
Fuel supply: Two horizontal SU carburettors
Suspension: Independent front, beam-axle rear
Weight: 1,328 lb
Top speed: 87 mph

By using Austin A35 and Morris Minor 1000 pieces (including a tuned-up version of the famous 948 cc engine), Donald and Geoffrey Healey produced a simple and rugged little two-seater, into which they built a great deal of sports car behaviour, and appealing character. Simple to the point of being rather starkly-equipped at first, the Sprite cut costs to the bone by specifying plastic side curtains, and by making the soft-top a simple item with a build-it-yourself frame.

No sooner was the new car launched, of course, than its unique styling, with

headlamps grafted on to the top of the bonnet panel, inspired the affectionate nickname of 'Frog Eye' (or, in the USA, 'Bug Eye'). This, however, was a feature forced upon the company at a late stage. Prototypes had fold-back headlamps designed to preserve a smooth line, but cost considerations forced a change to the fixed position on production cars. The entire bonnet/front wings assembly was hinged at the passenger bulkhead, and could be lifted up for access to the engine bay and front suspension assemblies. The result was a car which lacked aerodynamic purity, but had unmistakable looks. Perhaps by chance, it also made this car look 'cute': when added to its undeniable performance and spirited handling, this was a great marketing advantage.

The new Sprite was instantly a great success, especially in North America, where British sports cars were in great demand; over the next few years it also gained a reputation in sports car racing. Engine tune-up kits, suspension modifications and even special bodywork all helped to make it a successful race car.

In three years, no fewer than 48,987 'Frog Eye' Sprites were built, but this was only the beginning of a long success story. A restyled Mk II, with more conventional looks, then took over, and a near-identical MG Midget was also introduced; these cars then continued to sell at a phenomenal rate until the end of the 1970s. All in all, nearly 356,000 cars in this family were built, and every survivor is now revered as an affordable classic.

Above and below: This was a popular two-seater sports car designed by BMC which used many exisiting parts and which was easy to maintain.

1958 Lotus Elite

Right from the start, when he built his original special-bodied Austin Seven trials car, Colin Chapman showed signs of engineering genius. Setting up Lotus, he sold his first car kits in the early 1950s, and soon progressed to building advanced racing sports cars. The first true Lotus road car, however, was the very advanced Lotus Elite.

First shown in 1957, but not available until a year later, the new two-seater Elite coupé was irresistibly attractive. Even though Lotus was still a small company, Chapman had laid out a car which pushed technology to the limit. In particular, he decided to make the Elite without a separate chassis, using a fully-stressed fibreglass monocoque body which would only include steel sections for a few local reinforcements.

Not only was this amazing machine to be powered by a race-proved overhead-camshaft engine from Coventry-Climax, and had four-wheel independent suspension, but it was achingly beautiful, and was quite amazingly light in weight. No-one, it seems, was ever likely to confuse the Elite with any other car, for its tiny, smooth and always curving lines had no rivals. Looking back into history, its only real drawback was that the door windows could not be wound down, but had to be removed to provide better ventilation.

In engineering terms, though, 'adding lightness' often adds cost too, and there was no doubt that the Elite was always going to be a costly car to make and sell. The fibreglass monocoque body shells proved to be difficult to make in numbers, major bought-in items like the Coventry-Climax engine were very expensive, and owners soon found that a great deal of maintenance and loving

care was needed to keep the new sports car running. Refinement was not then a word which Lotus understood and the Elite was a rather crudely equipped and finished machine at first; the interior environment was very noisy, for there was little attempt to insulate the drive line and suspension fixings from the monocoque, which acted like a fully matured sound box.

As the years passed, the Elite's specification changed, with the power of the engine gradually being pushed up to 100 bhp (which brought the top speed to more than 120 mph, quite amazing for a 1.2-litre car), a ZF gear-box adapted and (for Series II cars) a different type of rear suspension geometry specified.

Lotus Elite

Years in production: 1958–62
Structure: Front engine/rear-drive. Fibreglass monocoque body/chassis
Engine type: 4-cylinder, single-overhead-camshaft
Bore and stroke: 76.2 x 66.6 mm
Capacity: 1,216 cc
Power: 83 bhp @ 6,250 rpm
Fuel supply: Two horizontal SU carburettors
Suspension: Independent front, independent rear
Weight: 1,455 lb
Top speed: 118 mph

Special Elites, particularly when prepared at the factory, were outstandingly successful class cars in GT racing, even appearing with honour in major events such as the Le Mans 24 Hour and Nurburgring Six Hour events. Years later Colin Chapman admitted that the Elite had never made profits for Lotus, which may explain why he was happy to phase it out in 1962, ahead of the arrival of the backbone chassised Elan. Nothing can ever detract from the gracious style and inventive engineering which went into the car. A total of 988 Elites were made.

Below: Committed owners usually forgave the Elite for the car's failings, as here was a car which drove and handled like no other rival. Light by the standards of the day, it was not only fast, but remarkably economical too.

1959 Triumph Herald

Compared with the dumpy Standard Eights and Tens which it replaced, the Triumph Herald was a totally different type of car. Stylish where the old Standards had been dull, and technically exciting where old Standards had been boring, the Herald was the first of a big family of saloons and sports cars which sold hugely for more than ten years.

In 1957 the Herald's design (which was masterminded by Harry Webster) came together quickly, and by happenstance. Standard-Triumph wanted to build a conventional replacement for the Standard Eight/Ten using the same running gear, but could find no supply of unit-construction body shells. Electing to revert to separate-frame construction, they then hired the prodigious young Italian, Giovanni Michelotti, to style the car, which he did, with great flair. From there, it was a short step to adopting all-independent suspension, an unbeatable tight turning circle (which could match the best of London taxis), to decide to construct the body from bolt-up major sections, and to engineer a whole series of derivatives – saloon, coupé, estate car and van – on the same basis.

In their class, the original Heralds had competitive performance, but it was their styling which gave them a marketing advantage over their rivals, where cars like the Ford Anglia and (soon) the Vauxhall Viva looked ordinary by comparison; the major rival, of course, was the Mini, which no other car in the world could match.

Eventually, there would be more variety: somehow a six-cylinder engine was shoe-horned into place, producing the Vitesse, while a shortened chassis, with impeccable Michelotti styling, became the Spitfire (4-cylinder) and GT6 (fastback 6-cylinder) sports cars. This was an entirely new venture for Standard-Triumph, and early problems were inevitable. Original 948 cc Heralds were perhaps overweight, and too expensive, their handling often seeming suspect, but steady improvement produced the larger-engined Herald 1200 in 1961, the car became increasingly popular in the mid 1960s.

Although the Herald saloons and convertibles were always the best sellers in this range, it was the Spitfire (for glamour) and the Vitesse (for smooth six-cylinder character) which added the gloss to an already successful image. Since this was also a time when the TR sports car was at the height of its fame, Triumph had an extremely good image in the 1960s, which the Herald did much to support.

Lasting fame was assured even before the final Heralds were made in 1971, for by this time they were 13/60s with 1.3-litre engines, and were the last separate-chassis cars on UK sale. In later years, particularly in sporting form, they became much-loved classics.

Triumph Herald

Years in production: (All types) 1959–71
Structure: Front engine/rear-drive. Separate chassis
Engine type: 4-cylinder, overhead-valve
ORIGINAL 948 CC TYPE:
Bore and stroke: 63 x 76 mm
Capacity: 948 cc
Power: 34.5/45 bhp @ 4,500/5,800 rpm
Fuel supply: Single Solex/two horizontal SU carburettors
Suspension: Independent front, independent rear
Weight: 1,764 lb
Top speed: 71 mph/79 mph

Left and below: A totally different type of car, the Herald was designed by the Italian Michelotti with great flair, and sold in huge numbers for more than ten years. Their individual style gave them a significant marketing advantage over their rivals.

1959 Austin-Healey 3000

Mention the famous phrase 'Big Healey', and someone will automatically add 'hairy–chested' to the description. Originally announced in 1952 as a beautiful two-seater sports car using a four-cylinder Austin A90 engine, this was a car which would grow larger, heavier, faster and more characterful in a full 15-year career. The last of the famous line was the Austin-Healey 3000, which went on sale in 1959.

The original 'Healey 100' began as a private venture from Donald Healey's small company, and was supposed to use Austin/BMC running gear. However, as soon as that company's chairman, Len Lord, saw the car, he tied up a deal with Healey – that the car would be manufactured by BMC at Longbridge, that its name would be changed, and that the Healey company would be retained as sports car design consultants thereafter. First deliveries of Austin-Healey 100s followed in 1953.

From 1952 to 1956 these four-cylinder cars sold well, especially in the USA. They were then re-engineered with BMC's new six-cylinder engine, becoming the '100 Six'. Three years later, with an enlarged engine, the same cars were rebadged as the '3000', which it remained for the next eight years. In 1957 final assembly was moved to the MG factory at Abingdon, two-seater or 2+2-seat options were made available, along with optional hard-tops, optional overdrive, single or duo-tone colour schemes, and a mass of accessories.

Earlier cars were raced at Le Mans and Sebring, and were used in a number of high-profile long distance record attempts. Healey produced more and more, performance-raising options. By the 1960s in much-modified and 'works' prepared form, the 3000 was a formidable rally car, and a good sports car racer, its most famous achievement when Pat Moss (Stirling's sister) won the gruelling Liège-Rome-Liège Rally of 1960.

If standard production types had a problem, it was that they were a little too low slung, and that they passed far too much engine heat into the cockpit, but in view of their style, their performance and their character, enthusiasts forgave them everything. From 1962, in any case, the body was re-engineered with wind-up windows and a curved screen, while from 1964 the interior was also rejigged and the ground clearance raised.

The last of all, the Mk IIIs, were the best. In total, there were more than 58,000 six-cylinder engined cars, and more than 73,000 of all types.

Austin-Healey 3000

Years in production: (All 3000s) 1959–68
Structure: Front engine/rear-drive. Separate chassis
Engine type: 6-cylinder, overhead-valve
Bore and stroke: 83.34 x 88.9 mm
Capacity: 2,912 cc
Power: 124 bhp @ 4,600 rpm – latterly 148 bhp @ 5,250 rpm
Fuel supply: Two horizontal SU carburettors
Suspension: Independent front, beam-axle rear
Weight: 2,465 lb
Top speed: 114 mph (latterly 121 mph)

Below: Every six-cylinder car had the same butch character, made all the right noises when pressed hard, and had the same sort of rugged dependability which sports car enthusiasts enjoyed.

1959 Austin-Morris Mini

Announced in 1959, and still manufactured 40 years later at the end of the century, Alec Issigonis's cheeky little Mini-Minor changed the face of motoring. The world's first car to combine front-wheel-drive and a transversely-mounted engine in a tiny ten-foot long package, was the most efficient and effective use of road space that had ever been seen. In so many ways, this must qualify as the 'car of the century'.

In scheming up the car Issigonis and his team, which had already designed the Morris Minor, was given a difficult brief by the British Motor Corporation. In the aftermath of the Suez Crisis, and threatened world-wide petrol rationing, Issigonis was asked to provide a minimum-size, minimum-price four-seater package – all built around an

Austin-Morris Mini

Years in production: Introduced 1959
Structure: Front engine/front-drive. Monocoque body/chassis
Engine type: 4-cylinder, overhead-valve
Bore and stroke: 62.94 x 68.26 mm
Capacity: 848 cc
Power: 34 bhp @ 5,500 rpm
Fuel supply: One horizontal SU carburettor
Suspension: Independent front, independent rear
Weight: 1,380 lb
Top speed: 72 mph

existing BMC engine. Choosing front-wheel-drive and the A-series engine, he then minimised the size of the car by turning the engine sideways, and mounted the transmission under the engine. Tiny (10 in /254 mm) diameter road wheels, independent suspension by rubber cone springs, and a careful packaging of the cabin, all helped to provide one of the most amazing little cars of all time. So what if the driving position was cramped, and the steering wheel too vertical? This was a Mini, after all.

Although Issigonis insisted that he was only providing a super-small, super-economy saloon, almost by chance his Mini had superb handling, precise race-car-like steering and unmatched agility. Even before more powerful versions were available, the Mini had started winning rallies, and showing well in saloon car racing: later, in Mini-Cooper S form, size-for-size it was unbeatable.

Engines were eventually enlarged, tiny front-wheel disc brakes were added, the Mini-Cooper and Mini-Cooper S followed, and by the mid-1960s this was a car which had won the Monte Carlo Rally on several occasions. For years there was nothing a Mini could not do, for it appealed to everyone, and every social class, from royalty to the dustman, bought one. At peak, production in two factories (Longbridge and Cowley) exceeded 300,000 every year, BMC's only problem being that it was priced so keenly that profit margins were wafer thin.

Even the arrival of the larger Mini Metro in 1980 could not kill off the Mini, whose charm was unique. By the 1980s, with larger wheels, re-equipped interiors and wind-up windows, the Mini was a better car than ever, and, looking much the same, it was still selling steadily at the end of the 1990s: more than five million had already been made.

In 1994 BMW took control of the Rover group but by 2000 Rover were still suffering from massive losses. BMW let MG and Rover go to Phoenix a British consortium and sold off the remaining Minis that had been produced at the Birmingham plant. BMW kept hold of the Mini brand name and in 2001 their version of the Mini One and Mini Cooper were launched and have become a sales success throughout Europe and the US.

Far left: The steering wheel was nearly vertical in the little Mini.
Left The Suez Crisis led to the need for a small, economical saloon.
Below: The new style MINI Cooper produced by the UK subsidiary of BMW.

1959 Jaguar 3.8 Mk II

To see a Mk II in action these days, merely switch on the TV and watch any recycled British 'cops and robbers' programme of the 1960s and 1970s. If the police are not using one as a pursuit car, the 'baddies' will be driving one as a getaway car. One car, at least, is usually crashed in every episode – so it is a miracle that many have survived!

For the first ten post-war years, Jaguar produced only sports cars or big saloons with separate chassis frames: the 2.4 of 1955 was the first Jaguar to have a unit-construction body shell. This was the first of a large family of 'compact' four-door saloons which would follow in the next 13 years.

Although the original 2.4/3.4 types were rather dumpily styled, with thick windscreens and window surrounds, the Mk II versions which followed in 1959, were altogether more graceful. Styled by Jaguar's founder, Sir William Lyons, the Mk II built on the theme of the Mk I,

Jaguar 3.8 Mk II

Years in production: 1959–67
Structure: Front engine/rear-drive. Monocoque body/chassis
Engine type: 6-cylinder, twin-over head-camshaft
Bore and stroke: 87 x 106 mm
Capacity: 3,781 cc
Power: 220 bhp @ 5,500 rpm
Fuel supply: Two horizontal SU carburettors
Suspension: Independent front, beam-axle rear
Weight: 3,304 lb
Top speed: 125 mph

but had a larger window area, a wraparound rear window, lighter detailing, and an improved chassis, with a wider choice of equipment. The original front engine/rear-drive layout was retained, along with a beam rear axle retained by cantilever leaf springs. The latest cars had a much wider wheel track and handled much better than earlier models. Four-wheel disc brakes had been standardised, so they also felt much safer too.

Most importantly, Mk IIs were available with a choice of XK six-cylinder engines – 2.4-litre, 3.4-litre and 3.8-litre types – along with manual, overdrive, or automatic transmission, disc or wire spoke wheels, and a raft of desirable extras. With Jaguar sales rising past 500 cars every week, the choice seemed endless.

As the years passed, Daimler V8-engined versions also appeared, as did the long-tail S-type (which had independent rear suspension), the 420 of 1966 being the final version. Predictably, the most glamorous Mk IIs were the 3.8-litre types, which were amazingly powerful and flexible, preferably built in a bright colour (fire engine red was popular, for instance), with overdrive transmission and chrome-plated wire-spoke wheels. Not only were they exciting 125 mph cars, virtually peerless in open road use, but they were thoroughly practical and versatile four-seater saloons as well.

Unleashing the booming straight-line performance was one thing, but controlling it was quite another; radial ply tyres were still rare, and tyre grip was, in any case, primitive. To drive a Mk II fast on twisty, slippery roads required supreme skill – for it could bite back swiftly. A well prepared Mk II, however, was a formidable racing saloon car, unbeatable for years except by vast-engined American saloons. From 1959 until 1968, when it finally gave way to the XJ6, it was one of the most enjoyable and affordable sports saloons.

Left and above: A common sight in old movies, these graceful cars were the first in a series of large four-door saloons. The Mk II had a larger window area, a wraparound rear window and a wider choice of equipment than its predecessor.

1961 Jaguar E-type

By almost any reckoning, Jaguar's original E-type was the sexiest motor car ever launched. It looked wonderful, it was extremely fast, and it was always sold at extremely attractive prices. For more than a decade, it was the sports car by which all other supercar manufacturers had to measure themselves.

Originally conceived in 1956 as a successor to the D-type racing sports car, the E-type was not to be used for that purpose. Re-engineered and re-developed, it became an outstanding road-going sports car, taking over from the last of the XK cars – the XK150 – in 1961. Like the D-type, its structure acknowledged all the best contemporary aerospace principles, utilising a multi-tubular front chassis frame which surrounded the engine and supported the front suspension and steering, and was bolted up to the bulkhead of the pressed steel monocoque centre and rear end.

Power came from the very latest version of the famous XK six-cylinder twin-cam engine, with three SU carburettors and no less than 265 bhp (according to American SAE ratings). It was matched by all-independent suspension, four-wheel disc brakes, and a unique, wind-cheating body style. As with the C- and D-type racing cars, the E-type's shape had been designed by ex-aircraft industry specialist Malcolm Sayer, who combined great artistic flair for a line with the ability to calculate how the wind would flow over a car's contours. For practical purposes, the E-type's nose might have been too long,

Right: Considered to be the sexiest car ever launched, the E-type was a fast and outstanding sports car. Designed by an ex-aircraft specialist, it had a remarkable aerodynamic performance.

its cabin cramped, and its tail too high to hide all of the chassis components, but all this was forgiven by its remarkable aerodynamic performance – and its enormous visual appeal.

Open and fastback two-seaters were available from the start, and although a 150 mph top speed was difficult for an ordinary private owner to achieve, this was a supercar in all respects, being faster than any other British road car of the period (and, for that matter, for many years to come). Much-modified types eventually won a series of motor races at just below world level, for they were really too heavy for this purpose. Only three years after launch, a 4.2-litre engine, allied to a new synchromesh gearbox, was adopted, and a longer wheelbase 2+2 coupé followed in 1966.

The E-type sold well all around the world, especially in the USA although new safety laws caused the car to lose its power edge, and its headlamp covers before the end of the 1960s. The Series II's performance did not match that of the original, and by 1971, the E-type was a somewhat emasculated car. A final Series III type was powered by Jaguar's new 5.3-litre V12 engine, and a top speed of 150 mph was once again within reach.

Drivers did not seem to mind the small cabin and less than perfect ventilation, but in the end it was more safety regulations and changes in fashion that caused this wonderful motoring icon to fade away. The last of 72,520 E-types was built in 1975, when it was replaced by an entirely different type of sporting Jaguar, the larger, heavier and not so beautiful XJ-S.

Jaguar E-type

Years in production: (all types) 1961–75
Structure: Front engine/rear-drive. Monocoque body/chassis, tubular front chassis
ORIGINAL CARS:
Engine type: 6-cylinder, twin-overhead-camshaft
Bore and stroke: 87 x 106 mm
Capacity: 3,781 cc
Power: 265 bhp @ 5,500 rpm
Fuel supply: 3 horizontal SU carburettors
Suspension: Independent front, independent rear
Weight: 2,688 lb
Top speed: 149 mph

1962 AC Cobra

Here was the most extrovert sports car of all, British-built but with American V8 power. No-one ever bought a Cobra and expected to remain anonymous, for almost everything it did was noisy, flamboyant and spectacular.

In 1961 the former American racing driver, Carroll Shelby, approached AC, suggesting that they should supply Ace body/chassis assemblies to him in California, where he would insert Ford-USA V8 engines and transmissions for sale in the USA. AC, whose Ace was in any case approaching the end of its career, was delighted to do this business. In future years there would be arguments about the car's design provenance, its source, and even its true name. Everyone now knows it as a Cobra, but the Americans always wanted to call it a Shelby American Cobra, while the British insisted on their right to retain the famous AC badge.

In many ways the first Cobra was a thoroughly re-engineered Ace, which retained the same twin-tube chassis frame, all-independent suspension (by transverse leaf springs), and sleek aluminium-panelled 'Barchetta' style body. Compared with the Ace though, the tubular chassis was much stronger, there was a massive new rear axle, four-wheel disc brakes, and flares over the wheel arches to cover wider wheels and tyres.

Soon after deliveries began, a 4.7-litre V8 engine replaced the original 4.2-litre type, while rack-and-pinion steering was also standardised. Helped along by its extrovert character, and by a flamboyant motor racing programme which eventually saw the Cobras beating Ferrari production sports cars, it became a cult car in 1960s America. Shelby even went so far as to develop the Daytona Cobra race cars, with a dramatically different fastback coupé style, extremely rare cars which won the 1965 World Sports Car Championship.

On the road, a Cobra never did anything by halves, bellowing when the accelerator pedal was pressed, squealing its tyres at any excuse, and generally looking impressive and aggressive. All this was eventually tempered by technical improvements, for from 1965 a new chassis with coil spring suspension took over, wheel tracks were further widened (with body styling modified to suit), and an even more powerful version, the 7-litre powered Cobra 427, joined the range.

Production of the original Cobra (which was also sold in the UK as the AC 289) eventually ran out in 1968 after 1,137 cars had been made. This was by no means the end of a complicated saga however. In the 1970s enterprising specialists all over the world pirated the design, marketing what they called Cobra 'replicas' (though this transgression was speedily seen off by AC's lawyers). AC's successor company started building cars again in small numbers, and in the 1990s Carroll Shelby himself reactivated a series of unallocated original chassis plates to build new-old Cobras once again.

Many more Cobras, or so-called Cobras, now exist than were ever originally constructed in the 1960s, all them having the same sort of extrovert character as the originals. Although the name had changed, the Cobra's pedigree had not died away and, when it does, be sure that it will not go quietly.

Left and below: A British built car with Ford-USA V8 engines, the Cobra was to become a cult car in 1960s America. With the 4.7-litre V8 engine it was able to beat Ferrari production sports cars.

AC Cobra

Years in production: 1962-present
Structure: Front engine/rear-drive. Separate chassis
Engine type: V8-cylinder, overhead-valve
ORIGINAL AC 289:
Bore and stroke: 101.6 x 73 mm
Capacity: 4,727 cc
Power: 195 bhp @ 4,400 rpm
Fuel supply: One vertical Ford carburettor
Suspension: Independent front, independent rear
Weight: 2,315 lb
Top speed: 138 mph

1963 Aston Martin DB5

Fame comes in strange and unexpected ways. Although the Aston DB4 and DB5 models were already respected by the cognoscenti, the DB5 did not become world-famous until used as James Bond's personal transport in the film *Goldfinger*. Although not equipped with Bond's ejector seat, it appealed to millions, and the DB5's reputation was secure for ever. Technically, of course, Aston Martin had always been a marque of distinction.

Following the success of the DB2, DB2/4 and DB Mk III models of the 1950s, Aston Martin commissioned a totally new and larger series for the 1960s, beginning with the DB4 in 1958. Built around a simple steel platform chassis, it was clothed in a sleek light-alloy fastback body style by Superleggera Touring of Italy (but built at Newport Pagnell). The skin panels were fixed to a network of light tubing, a method patented by Superleggera. Power (and what power!) came from a magnificent new 3.7-litre twin-cam six-cylinder engine, which soon proved to be strong and reliable in motor racing. The DB4 came close to matching anything so far achieved by Ferrari. All this, allied to a close-coupled four-seater cabin, and high (traditionally British) standards of trim and equipment, made the expensive DB4 very desirable.

The DB5, which was launched in 1963, was a direct development of the DB4; it had a full 4-litre engine, a more rounded nose with recessed-headlamps, and many equipment improvements. Two varieties of engine – the most powerful with a claimed 314 bhp – were on offer, as were non-sporting options such as automatic transmission, which came a full decade before Ferrari stooped to such action.

It was such a complicated, mainly hand-built, machine that it had to sell at high prices. The saloon cost an eye-watering £4,175 in 1963 (there was also a convertible version, at £4,490) and because assembly was a lengthy and careful business, sales were limited to only ten cars a week. It was not for years, incidentally, that it became

clear that even these prices did not cover costs, for Aston Martin was merely the industrial plaything of its owner, tractor magnate David Brown.

DB5s could safely reach 140 mph, with roadholding, steering and brakes to match, all the time producing the characteristic booming exhaust notes for which they became famous. Although they looked sinuous and dashing, they were heavy machines and there was no power-assisted steering on this model.

Clearly, this was a bespoke GT machine which would run and run, as the longer and more spacious DB6 which took over in 1965 would prove. In only two years, a total of 1,063 cars (123 convertibles, and 12 of them very special estate car types) were produced. Almost all have survived.

Aston Martin DB5

Years in production: 1963–65
Structure: Front engine/rear-drive. Platform separate chassis
Engine type: 6-cylinder, twin-over head-camshaft
Bore and stroke: 96 x 92 mm
Capacity: 3,995 cc
Power: 282/314 bhp @ 5,500 rpm
Fuel supply: Three horizontal SU/3 dual-choke Weber carburettors
Suspension: Independent front, beam-axle rear
Weight: 3,235 lb
Top speed: 141 mph

Left, above and right: The DB5 became world-famous as James Bond's car in the film Goldfinger. *Lacking the ejector seat, this mainly hand-built car appealed to millions. Although it was a heavy car to drive, as it lacked power-assisted steering, the DB5 had good roadholding, control and brakes to match.*

1963 Hillman Imp

Hillman's rear-engined Imp, launched in 1963 and built until the mid-1970s, was the right car at the wrong time. If it had not had to compete with BMC's well established Mini, and if it had not been made by a financially ailing Rootes group, it could have been a great success. The design, in other words, was much more successful than its sales.

For the Rootes Group, already famous for building a series of conventional Hillmans, Humbers and Sunbeams, the decision to develop a new small car was extremely brave. Having looked closely at cars like the Mini, the Ford Anglia and the Triumph Herald, Rootes cast convention to the winds and opted for a rear-engined car – the 'Apex' project.

The engine was located in the tail, and the transmission ahead of it. This meant developing a new alloy engine (which was based on a Coventry-Climax racing design), transmission and all-independent suspension layout. Swing axle front suspension, and semi-trailing arms at the rear were remarkably effective, much of the luggage was stowed up front, but there was also space behind the rear seats, ahead of the engine.

Functionally, the new 'Apex' (which would

Hillman Imp
Years in production: 1963–76
Structure: Rear engine/rear-drive. Monocoque body/chassis
Engine type: 4-cylinder, single overhead camshaft
Bore and stroke: 68 x 60.4 mm
Capacity: 875 cc
Power: 37 bhp @ 4,800 rpm
Fuel supply: One downdraught Solex
Suspension: Independent front, independent rear
Weight: 1,530 lb
Top speed: 78 mph

eventually carry Hillman, Singer, Sunbeam and Commer badges) was advanced and successful. The style of the saloons was craggy in the extreme (the rear-engined Chevrolet Corvair was thought to be an inspiration), but it was much more roomy than the Mini, and had a useful lift-up rear window feature. Though the Imp's weight was heavily biased towards the rear, the handling was remarkably good, the steering inch-perfect, and the traction superb. If only the first cars' reliability had been better, and the prices a little lower, the Imp might have successfully established itself.

The problem, however, was that for political and employment purposes, Rootes had been obliged to build Imps at a factory near Glasgow, in Scotland, with an inexperienced workforce, while engines and transmissions were assembled in the Midlands, and much shuffling of components ensued. To make a great car from this framework was almost impossible.

Early reliability problems were eliminated within two or three years, but in spite of a facelift, and the introduction of sporty versions, the Imp project always struggled to make its mark. Yet this was unwarranted. Singer types were much better furnished, Sunbeams had more powerful engines and 90 mph performance, while the fastback coupé versions (notably the Sunbeam Stiletto) were chic and well specified. A successful race and 'works' rally programme (which included success in the British Saloon Championship) helped underpin the image. More than 440,000 of all varieties were made before 1976. Now that these cars are retired, they have an enthusiastic following.

Above: The rear-engine design of Hillman Imp was a great success. However, due to the political pressure, Rootes built the car with an inexperienced Scottish workforce, which contributed to early reliability problems and undermined sales.

1964 Sunbeam Tiger

If the AC Cobra of 1962 was the first attempt to mate American V8 power with a British sports car chassis, the Sunbeam Tiger of 1964 was the first to tackle the same feat in quantity production. It was the same entrepreneur, Texan Carroll Shelby, whose engineers built the first of both versions, but in the case of the Tiger, final development was a joint effort between the British Rootes Group, and its subcontractors, Jensen.

Introduced in 1959, the Sunbeam Alpine was a stylish British sports car, which combined a short-wheelbase version of the Rapier's platform and running gear, with a very smart new two-seater sports car style. Compared with its rivals – the MGA and the Triumph TR3A – it was under-powered, so a proposal to fit a 4.2-litre Ford-USA V8 (and give the car a new title) looked like a great opportunity.

Rootes arranged for Pressed Steel to supply complete body shells to Jensen, who modified them as appropriate, and then assembled the whole cars. Announced early in 1964, the newly-named Tiger had the body style of the Alpine IV (in which the rear fins had been cut down, and the interior improved), and was available in soft-top or detachable hardtop form. In the first year, 1964–65, all supplies went to the USA, but the Tiger was put on sale in the UK from 1965.

With 164 bhp instead of the contemporary 1.6-litre Alpine's 82 bhp, the Tiger was a much fiercer proposition, which gave, as the Americans said, 'more bangs per buck', and soon began to build a following. It was the sort of car which seemed eager to spin its rear wheels – and many owners did just that. Unhappily, compared with the Alpine, there were only minor styling changes, and no opportunity was available to beef up the chassis, so Tiger customers soon found that the original type was not yet a completely balanced package.

Even so, a short-lived motor racing programme (two Tigers competed at Le Mans in 1964), and an altogether more successful 'works' rally programme began to promote the message that here was a car with performance and durability. All would have been well if Rootes, in the meantime, had not sold out to the Chrysler Corporation, who took an instant dislike to a car which was powered by the engine of one of its deadliest rivals.

Second thoughts are often better than the first, but although Rootes introduced the Tiger II in 1967, complete with a 200 bhp/4.7-litre engine and four-wheel disc brakes, Chrysler soon insisted that it be killed off and these rare, but fully-formed machines, became both the best, and least-known Tigers of all.

Sunbeam Tiger

Years in production: (All types) 1964–67
Structure: Front engine/rear-drive. Monocoque body/chassis
Engine type: V8-cylinder, over head-valve
Bore and stroke: 96.5 x 73 mm
Capacity: 4,261 cc
Power: 164 bhp @ 4,400 rpm
Fuel supply: One downdraught Ford carburettor
Suspension: Independent front, beam-axle rear
Weight: 2,525 lb
Top speed: 117 mph

Right and below: A stylish sports car, the Tiger's production halted when Chrysler bought Rootes, as the engine was powered by a rival company.

1966 Jensen FF and Interceptor

Established by the Jensen brothers in West Bromwich in the 1930s, Jensen's first cars were stylish, but otherwise technically mundane machines. Even by the 1950s and early 1960s their successors' appeal was more in what they looked like, than how they were equipped. Then, buoyed up by the profits from a great deal of contract work (Jensen built complete bodies for the Austin-Healey 3000, and tackled complete assembly of the Sunbeam Tiger sports car), the decision was taken to modernise. The result was the launch of two stunningly handsome four-seater coupés, known as the Interceptor and the FF.

Jensen Interceptor and FF

Years in production: (All types) 1966–76
Structure: Front engine/rear-drive (FF = four-wheel-drive). Separate chassis
Engine type: V8-cylinder, over head-valve
ORIGINAL TYPE:
Bore and stroke: 108 x 86 mm
Capacity: 6,276 cc
Power: 325 bhp @ 4,600 rpm
Fuel supply: One downdraught Carter carburettor
Suspension: Independent front, beam-axle rear
Weight: 3,500 (FF = 4,030)lb
Top speed: 133 mph

Right and below: With Italian styling, the Jensen was a well-equipped coupé, easy to handle with a large expanse of glass. The introduction of anti-lock brakes and four-wheel drive was a massive technical breakthrough.

By combining the existing Jensen tubular chassis frame with a vast Chrysler V8 engine and automatic transmission, and swathing the whole in a body styled by Touring of Italy, the result was a modern-looking coupé, with graceful lines, a great deal of glass, and a well equipped cabin. This new Jensen, however, broke new ground, not just for Britain, but for the entire world of motoring. By

co-operating with Harry Ferguson Research, Jensen offered one version of the car, the FF, with four-wheel-drive. This, and the use of Dunlop Maxaret anti-lock braking, was a massive technical breakthrough.

To do all this, the drive was split behind the main gearbox, a second propeller shaft was threaded forward alongside the engine, and the car's wheelbase had to be stretched by four inches to accommodate a front axle ahead of the engine. By modern standards the installation looked crude, but it was a world 'first', and remarkably effective.

The FF was much more expensive than its rear-drive cousin: in 1966 the UK prices were £5,340 and £3,743, at a time when a new Rolls-Royce cost £6,670, and sales were always limited. It was the Interceptor which sold in quantity and helped give Jensen an entirely new image.

Not only were these very fast cars (an Interceptor could reach 133 mph, and an FF about 130 mph), but they were also easy to handle, enjoyable grand tourers in spite of their bulk. By the time the specification had settled down, they had power-assisted steering, were effortless to drive, and the equipment had received two upgrades. Demand was strong.

Although only 320 FFs were made before production closed down in 1971, the older the Interceptor became, the faster it sold. By the mid-1970s one version, powered by a 385 bhp Chrysler engine, could reach 145 mph, while convertible and hard-top versions added to the variety.

Unhappily, the after effects of the 1973 Energy Crisis, and Jensen's other problems connected with the Jensen-Healey dragged down the Interceptor, which died in 1976 after 6,639 cars had been produced. Later attempts to revive the Interceptor, first in the 1980s, and then in the 1990s, both failed.

1970 Range Rover

Rover never hid the fact that their original Land Rover 4x4, which went on sale in 1948, was inspired by the famous US military Jeep. The Range Rover of 1970, however, was unique. Bigger, heavier, better equipped than any previous Land Rover, it opened up an entirely new type of market. Although it was conceived simply as a 'bigger Land Rover', even before it went on sale it had become more of a gentleman's 4x4, and less of an all-can-do workhorse, and that process carried on inexorably over the next 25 years. By the time the last Range Rover 'Classic' was produced in 1995, no fewer than 317,615 had been built.

The first Range Rovers had a 100 in (2540 mm) wheelbase, were powered by a de-tuned version of Rover's ex-GM V8 engine, had a newly-engineered four-wheel-drive layout, and their beam front and rear axles ran on long-travel coil springs. Not only did the light-alloy-clad estate car body shell look smart, but this was also a vehicle with quite unrivalled on- or off-road abilities.

Although Rover originally looked on the Range

Rover as a hard-working and versatile tool which could be used in the most awful conditions (which, indeed, it was, and could), they soon found that more and more customers were using it as a large, high-capacity, estate car which rarely left surfaced roads. Quips that Range Rovers rarely attempted anything more than wet gravel in a supermarket car park were met by Rover with broad smiles and the response: 'Look at the sales figures'.

Although the styling altered only slightly over the years, the specification advanced considerably. Automatic transmission, five forward speeds instead of four, and eventually a fuel-injected version of the engine were all added in the 1980s. A five-door body option within the same overall package was an instant best seller, limited-edition packs called 'Vogue' soon became regular options, while the specification, equipment, fittings and features all gradually increased.

Range Rover

Years in production: (First generation) 1970–95
Structure: Front engine/four-wheel-drive. Separate chassis
Engine type: V8-cylinder, overhead-valve
ORIGINAL TYPE
Bore and stroke: 88.9 x 71.1 mm
Capacity: 3,528 cc
Power: 135 bhp @ 4,750 rpm
Fuel supply: 2 SU carburettors
Suspension: Beam-axle front, beam-axle rear
Weight: 3,880 lb
Top speed: 99 mph

By the late 1980s the Range Rover was also available with a diesel engine option (which was much more popular in certain export markets and with businesses than ever it was with private British buyers), and before long the most expensive, highest-specified versions had 200 bhp 4.2-litre engines, longer wheelbase bodies and self-levelling suspensions. Early cars which had a top speed of 92 mph were quite outclassed by these machines, which could top 110 mph, though the fuel consumption was very heavy (worse than 15 mpg).

During the 1990s, the Land Rover Discovery appeared, using the original 'short' Range Rover chassis, and from 1994 there was a completely new-generation Range Rover, even faster, more expensive and glossier than ever before. In 20 years, the Range Rover had established an entirely new market sector which left its rivals struggling to catch up.

Left and above: Bigger and heavier than the Land Rover of 1948, the Range Rover was the first high capacity estate car, which preceded the explosion in 4x4 vehicles of the 1990s.

It is easy to recognise the 1958 Lotus Elite; its stream-lined design and smooth bodywork were unrivalled.

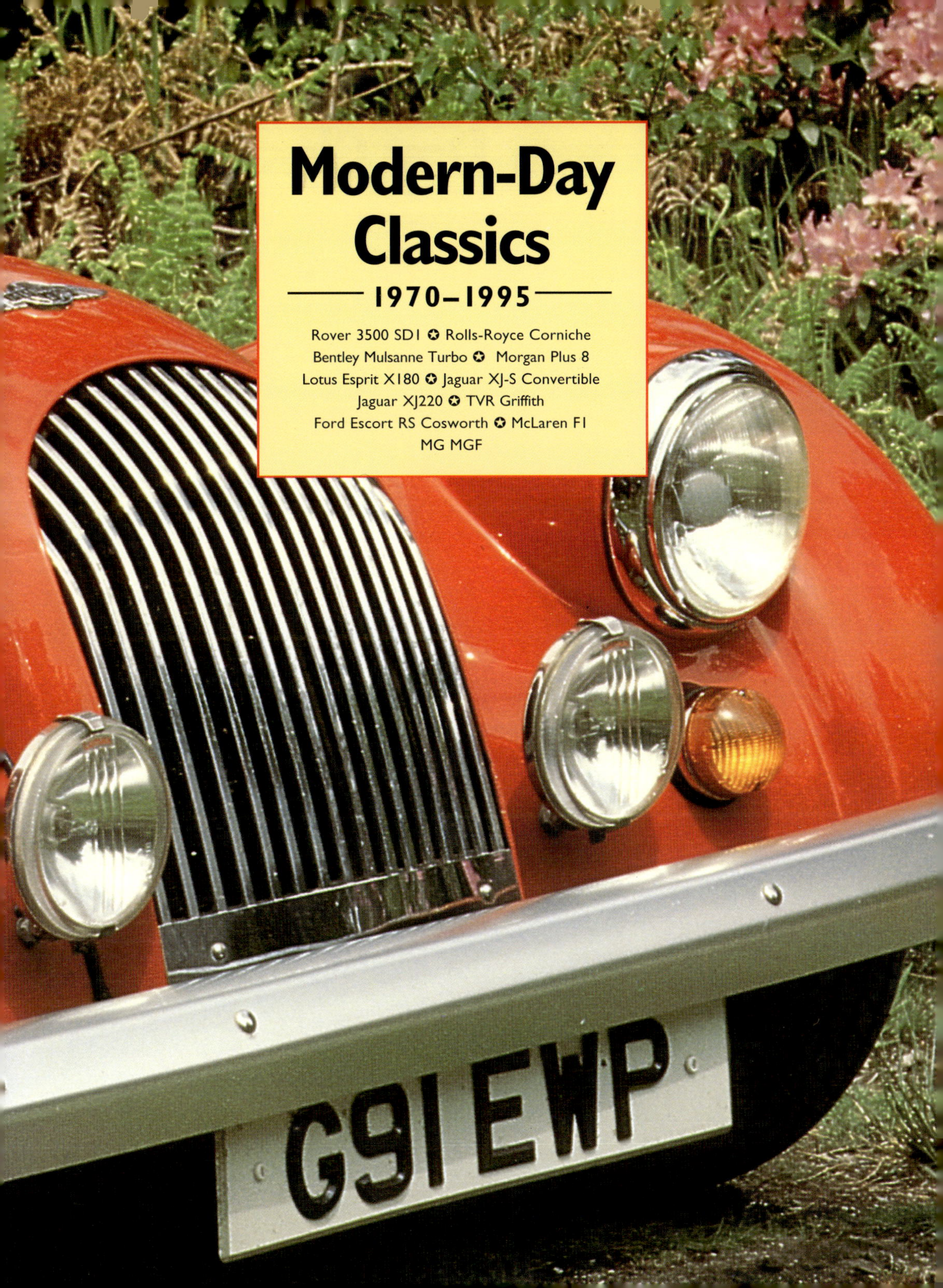

Modern-Day Classics

1970–1995

Rover 3500 SD1 ✪ Rolls-Royce Corniche
Bentley Mulsanne Turbo ✪ Morgan Plus 8
Lotus Esprit X180 ✪ Jaguar XJ-S Convertible
Jaguar XJ220 ✪ TVR Griffith
Ford Escort RS Cosworth ✪ McLaren F1
MG MGF

Modern-Day Classics

For British motorists in the late 1970s, the miracle was that the climate for motoring changed so fast. Even though there had been two vicious energy crises and a long period of horrifyingly high inflation, fine cars were still being made, space was still available to drive them, and new styles were still being developed. It was amazing. Only ten years after the first energy crisis had made most people fear for their future mobility, all the fun in motoring had returned. Maybe there were not as many sports cars as before, but high-performance saloons and hatchbacks seemed to be everywhere.

By the late 1980s, and following a long world-wide economic boom, Britain produced a series of magnificent supercars. Some, like the first Ford Sierra RS Cosworth, seemed easily affordable, while others, like the Jaguar XJ220, were merely there to be admired by many, but owned by very few. That didn't matter. By the 1980s and 1990s what truly mattered was that the definition of a 'classic' car altered. It was clear that there would be 'classics', 'modern classics' and 'sleepers'. Even better, cars came on to the market and were immediately hailed as 'instant classics' – the Bentley Mulsanne Turbo and the Ford Escort RS Cosworth being typical.

CONSOLIDATION

Car makers struggled to survive during the 1970s, and no important new marques were established. Some, like Lotus and TVR, made bigger, glossier and more costly models, but others, like AC, Jensen and even Triumph barely remained in business.

By the end of the decade British Leyland (which included Jaguar, MG and Rover) had gone bankrupt and then been nationalised, but otherwise the 'big four' looked stable, though more change was yet to come. Ford had established market leadership in the 1970s, BL (which soon became Austin-Rover) tucked in behind them, with Vauxhall and Peugeot-Talbot (who acquired the ex-Rootes, ex-Chrysler business in 1978) bringing up the rear. Without exception, they forged stronger links with overseas combines – Ford's move into Ford-of-

Below: The Rolls-Royce continued to be the best built car in the world using the highest quality materials and offering all important exclusivity.

Above: The TVR Griffith is symbolic of the continued survival and prosperity of the privately owned Blackpool car maker.

Europe being first, and BL's tie-up with Honda last – which meant that individual British characteristics were bound to fade away with time.

Individual companies, which survived in remarkable numbers, sometimes absolutely on their own, tried to retain their integrity. Aston Martin went through a series of rich, paternalistic, owners before finally selling out to Ford in 1987, while Jaguar broke loose of British Leyland in 1984 (the government privatised that side of the business) but were then absorbed by Ford in 1989. Lotus survived until 1982, when the founder Colin Chapman died, and when Toyota took a stake, though it wasn't until 1986 that General Motors took control. For a short time, too, Lotus had technical links with DeLorean, of Northern Ireland, though that enterprise collapsed in 1982, its proprietor accused of financial skullduggery. In and around all this, TVR survived and prospered by operating with only two benevolent owners in the technical backwater of seaside Blackpool.

Most car makers exercised caution. The sleek Jaguar E-type had given way to the craggy XJ-S. MG Midgets and MGBs were built for years after their appeal had faded, for British Leyland never planned any successors, and the rival TR7s were not good enough to supplant them. Ford Escort RS models gradually faded away. Other classics – Range Rover and Morgan among them – continued, apparently *ad infinitum*, their sponsors lacking the drive or the inclination to produce anything new. Then, in the 1980s, inflation was slashed and industrial optimism returned. Except for Jaguar, Britain's motor industry found that it could survive without the North American market, and that it could continue to design and build great cars that the rest of the world wanted to buy.

Jaguar's case history tells us so much about the period. By the mid-1970s their business was in disarray, the E-type dead, and their products criticised for poor build quality. The big cats roared back in the 1980s: the XJ-S matured with honour, special Jaguars won the Le Mans 24 Hour race (and later, the World Sports Car Championship), and from 1989 they received the benevolent and long-term backing of Ford. The XJ6 saloon was rejuvenated as the V8-engined XK8, and a new smaller car (the S-type) was added in 1999. In almost every case, 1980s and 1990s Jaguars were 'instant classics', as we will surely discover in the 2000s and beyond.

Lotus, too, had a hard time, but survived, albeit under their third (or was it their fourth?) owner since Colin Chapman's death. Poorly-built Esprits of the 1970s became re-styled and more powerful Esprit V8s for the 1990s. A bravely-engineered front-wheel-drive Elan project only failed because it was too costly, and in more recent times a super-light, super-sporting Elise two-seater sold in higher numbers than almost any previous Lotus. Pedigree and soul, it seems, will usually prevail.

In the case of Triumph and the 'classic' MG, it did not, but in the case of the revived MG, and Aston Martin, it did. In the 1970s Triumph continued to outsell MG, but both were eventually killed off when BL stopped making sports cars. Then came an astonishing re-birth. Two owners down the line (for BMW took control in 1994), the MG sports car was back, first as the disgracefully paunchy RV8, which was pastiche in every way, but later as the mid-engined MGF.

Here was a classic British car reborn, created by a team who clearly understood what the magic initials 'MG' and 'sports car' should mean. Like the MGAs and the MGBs of old, the car was built around existing saloon car parts (in this case, Rover 100/200/400 types), but with a unique style, sporty handling, and a great deal of character.

This was the sort of car on which British automobile engineers became increasing expert in the 1970s, 1980s and 1990s. They knew how to build character into a new model without letting costs run out of control, they knew that good handling cost no more than bad, and that beautiful lines were just as easy to manufacture as ugly ones. The problem, however, was that they were rarely allowed to prove it.

In some cases, as with the gently-changing family of Rolls-Royce and Bentley, cost was not such a cramping factor: build-quality and exclusivity were all-important. By that time, it was said, a Rolls-Royce was no longer the 'Best Car in the World' (which had once been their proud advertising claim), especially when performance and roadholding was taken into consideration, but it seemed that it was always the best built. No matter how hard their rivals (at home and overseas) tried, it seemed that these cars had the very best quality materials, were the most carefully built, were the most rigorously tested, and offered a unique package of virtues. 'What would happen if a sub-standard Rolls-Royce left the building ?' a spokesman was once asked. 'The security guard would never let it out of the gate', he replied without hesitation.

Cars produced by small bespoke companies such as Aston Martin could not quite approach Rolls-Royce standards (though their performance was usually much higher). Even in the 1970s and 1980s, when their commercial existence sometimes hung by a thread, Aston Martins were always fast, well presented, impressively and uniquely styled, with very high performance. Things actually improved at Aston Martin after Ford took over, for new models and new methods could be considered for the first time in many years. The new DB7 of 1994 (which had many Jaguar components hidden away) was immediately seen as more 'classic', more desirable and of even better value than before. It was this approach to making desirable cars which gave the British motor industry a lead over its rivals.

By the 1990s, however, 'instant classic' British cars were being produced for two different reasons – one because they had a single-purpose job to do, the other being that they had to offer the very pinnacle in automotive engineering. Some 'single-purpose' cars which, by defini-

Opposite page: The Ford Escort RS Cosworth of 1992 became a highly desirable, instant classic with four-wheel-drive and a turbo-charged engine derived directly from motor sport.

Above: The mid-engined MG MGF was the result of an astonishing rebirth of this classic car in 1994 and points the way forward for British car makers into the new millenium.

tion were 'outstandingly important', and therefore potentially of classic status, came along to satisfy motorsport regulations. This explains the series of fine limited-production Fords starting with the 200-off RS200 of 1985, and culminating in the four-wheel-drive Escort RS Cosworth of 1992. If a car needed four-wheel-drive, a turbocharged engine, and positive downforce to make it competitive, then it should have it, Ford concluded. If, along the way, it became highly desirable, this was a bonus.

Britain's two fastest-ever cars, the Jaguar XJ220 and the McLaren F1, were built for an entirely different reason. Each, in its own way, was meant to be the ultimate car. The XJ220 was built to meet a small and prestige-conscious market of millionaires, pop stars and playboys who wanted the biggest toys and were ready to pay for them. The McLaren F1 which followed was looking for the same clientele, but wanted to offer even more. Technically, both cars were a huge and instant-classic success, but commercially both were failures. They were aimed at a fragile market which could (and did) disappear, but both proved, without question, that British engineers could still provide superlative cars ahead of their competitors.

For the 21st century the prospects are good, and there could well be more cars like these. In spite of everything, it seems classic British motor cars will continue to appear, to be loved by motoring enthusiasts and to be revered as they grow old. Compared with earlier generations, however, almost all of them will be specialist models, built for a specific purpose. In all honesty, because of the stifling legislative climate, I cannot foresee a new generation of British family car ever attracting as much praise as the sheer breathtaking charm of a BMC Mini.

There will, on the other hand, certainly be great new Millennium cars to take over from the MGF, the McLaren F1 and from sumptuously hand-built cars like the Bentley Mulsanne Turbo. Each will probably fulfil a small, specific, but definite need, and will be distinct and desirable because of that. As one famous motoring personality said in the depths of a 1970s energy crisis: 'It doesn't matter what fuel we have to use, if the cars are still fun. I don't care if I have to feed a car Mars Bars to make it run, just as long as it makes me smile....'

1976 Rover 3500 SD1

In the post-war years, Rover's image changed considerably. First they built staid and dignified saloons, then Land Rover 4x4s were added to the range, they dabbled with gas-turbine powered cars, and finally turned to the technically advanced Rover 2000 range.

Taken over by Leyland in 1967, Rover carried the process a stage further and the launch of the 3500 confirmed an attempt to satisfy the mass market. Designed under the guidance of Spen King, the new 'SD1' (the acronym stood for 'Specialist Division, Project 1') was a big five-door hatchback which effectively took the place of two older cars – the Rover 2200/3500 range, and the Triumph 2000/2500.

Although the cabin was laid out as a five-seater, with a bench rear seat, in traditional Rover fashion it was really more comfortable as a four-seater.

Simpler than originally expected, the original car mated the well known light-alloy V8, in a front engine/rear-drive layout, with a well located beam rear axle. Faster and easier to handle than previous Rovers, the new 3500 made many friends as a sports saloon, but it also began to make enemies

Rover 3500 SD1

Years in production: (All types) 1976–86
Structure: Front engine/rear-drive. Monocoque body/chassis
Engine type: Various 4-cylinder/ 6-cylinder/V8-cylinder, petrol and diesel
ORIGINAL TYPE:
Bore and stroke: 88.9 x 71.1 mm
Capacity: 3,528 cc
Power: 155 bhp @ 5,250 rpm
Fuel supply: Two horizontal SU carburettors
Suspension: Independent front, beam-axle rear
Weight: 2,989 lb
Top speed: 123 mph

because of the quality problems which afflicted many British Leyland models of the period.

As with many modern cars, this Rover was not just one model, but a complete range, and by 1982 the original V8 had been joined by a 2-litre four, 2.3-litre and 2.6-litre six, and a 2.4-litre diesel power unit. By this time, too, final assembly had been moved from the original Rover plant in the Midlands to the British Leyland factory at Cowley, and the car had been treated to a subtle but definite styling facelift. British Leyland also dabbled with an estate car version, but although prototypes were seen in public, they never went on sale.

The Vitesse, the fastest SD1, was introduced at the end of 1982, with a 190 bhp fuel-injected version of the V8 engine. Complete with a vast rear spoiler, the Vitesse had a top speed of 132 mph, and outstanding roadholding to match. Before long, highly-tuned Vitesses were winning Touring Car races all over Europe, and it was not until special turbocharged Fords were introduced that they were regularly defeated.

Over the years, the SD1 built up a real following, especially among the racing fraternity, and V8 examples, particularly Vitesses, are still prized. 300,000 cars of all types were produced before the last were built in 1986.

Below: The style, which was influenced by existing Italian supercars, (the Ferrari Daytona in particular), was smoother and more elongated than any previous Rover, and with no obvious visual links to its predecessors.

1979 Rolls-Royce Corniche

When Rolls-Royce announced its ground-breaking Silver Shadow range in 1965, which had an all-in-one chassis-less four-door body shell, pessimists forecast the imminent end to special-bodied models. Coachbuilders who had found it easy to build coachwork for fitment to separate-chassis models found it almost impossible to work the same magic on cars with monocoque, or unit-construction structures, where pressings and welding had to take over from hand-crafting and simple construction.

Rolls-Royce, therefore, decided to invest heavily at their Mulliner Park Ward subsidiary, and performed this miracle themselves. Starting in 1966, and using the saloon's platform, they announced a sleek two-door saloon, following it in 1967 with a convertible version of the same car. Rolls-Royce and Bentley versions were both sold. Those cars, updated and more powerful, were rebadged as 'Corniche' models: although the saloon was dropped in 1980, the convertible sold steadily until the mid-1990s.

Mechanically, every Corniche was closely related to the Rolls-Royce four-door saloon of the day – Silver Shadows until 1980, Silver Spirits thereafter – which is to say that they

Rolls-Royce Corniche

Years in production: (All types) 1971–94
Structure: Front engine/rear-drive. Monocoque body/chassis
Engine type: V8-cylinder, over head-valve
Bore and stroke: 104.1 x 99.1 mm
Capacity: 6,750 cc
Power: Not revealed
Fuel supply: Two horizontal SU carburettors/Bosch fuel injection
Suspension: Independent front, independent rear
Weight: 4,816 lb
Top speed: 120 mph

used 6.75-litre V8 engines, automatic transmission, self-levelling suspension and full power braking. Power, never officially revealed, was always described as 'adequate', and was enough to give the cars a top speed of around 120mph. The two-door coachwork was smooth and dignified, fitted out and finished to every expected Rolls-Royce standard, with leather seating, a wooden fascia panel, deep pile carpets, and a full array of instruments and controls. Automatic air-conditioning was standard – even in convertibles which might be expected to be used hood-down, on many occasions.

Although this was a thoroughly and carefully developed motor car, the Corniche was not a machine to be used day in and day out, but was really a rich man's indulgence. It could take him far and fast in great luxury, in every climate. Somehow, it seemed, it was most at home on a Riviera boulevard, or on Rodeo Drive in Los Angeles.

The convertible version was topped off by a sumptuously detailed and furnished power-operated soft-top which covered the spacious four-seater interior. Such was the company's attention to detail that it regularly took up to two weeks to manufacture, fit and adjust before new cars could be delivered.

Chassis improvements paralleled those of the saloons, but from 1979 the platform, and particularly the rear suspension, was upgraded to the new Silver Spirit level, making the cars even more silent and dignified than before. From 1984 the Bentley version was re-badged as a Continental, though without mechanical changes. Then, as later, Rolls-Royce put ride comfort ahead of roadholding – it was always more comfortable to drive a Corniche in a measured manner than to try to hurry along.

In a good year, more than 200 Corniches would be made, and almost 6,000 convertibles were produced in 23 years.

Below: The convertible version of the Corniche two-door saloon had a power-operated soft-top, as well as automatic air-conditioning and leather seating.

1982 Bentley Mulsanne Turbo

By the 1980s, Bentley's original sporting pedigree was long forgotten. The big 'vintage' sports cars designed by W.O. Bentley in the 1920s had long gone, for Rolls-Royce had bought up the bankrupt company in 1931. Thereafter, new Bentleys ('Rolls-Bentleys' as they were often christened) became sporty versions of Rolls-Royce cars, though even this new pedigree was diluted as the years past. By the end of the 1970s, every Bentley characteristic, it seemed, had been extinguished, and sales were falling fast. Rolls-Royce's chief executive, David Plastow, then had a brainwave. After hiring Broadspeed to develop a turbocharged version of Rolls-Royce's vast V8 engine, he installed it in a Bentley Mulsanne saloon (which was really no more than a rebadged Rolls-Royce Silver Spirit), and the whole car was re-aligned as the ultimate millionaire's sports saloon.

When the new car, the Bentley Mulsanne Turbo, was launched in 1982, it caused a real stir. Faster than any existing Bentley or Rolls-Royce, the power output figure was not originally revealed although it is now known to have been 300 bhp. With a top speed of 135 mph and acceleration to match, this was a magnificent Bentley. The high-tech chassis, with self-levelling all-independent suspension and full-power brakes, and sumptuous trim, carpeting and equipment contributed to an irresistible, if expensive car.

Even though the first cars cost £58,613 (then, as later, they were among the most expensive new cars in the world) they immediately began to sell well. The fact that they held the road no better than other Rolls-Royces and Bentleys (for although the ride comfort was remarkable, the suspension and damping was still very soft) was no deterrent, for they provided an unrivalled level of high-speed comfort.

The Bentley Mulsanne Turbo, however, was only the first of a long line of turbocharged Bentleys, the last of which were still being made in the year 2000. The Bentley Turbo R of 1985 had much better roadholding, a fuel-injected engine was added a year later, suspension-adaptive damping was added for 1990 and a four-speed automatic transmission followed in 1991.

A whole series of sporty two-door versions also evolved from this chassis – notably the Continental R, the Azure convertible and the short-wheelbase Continental T. By that time, the venerable turbocharged 6.75-litre V8 engine produced up to 420 bhp, and some cars could reach 160 mph. By the end of the 1990s, well over 8,000 turbocharged Bentleys in this family had been sold.

Right: An irresistible millionaire's car, the Mulsanne Turbo sold well from its launch, despite its vast price. Superbly equipped, the car provided an unrivalled level of high speed comfort.

Bentley Mulsanne Turbo

Years in production: (All versions) 1982–98
Structure: Front engine/rear-drive. Monocoque body/chassis
Engine type: V8-cylinder, overhead-valve
Bore and stroke: 104.1 x 99.1 mm
Capacity: 6,750 cc
ORIGINAL VERSION:
Power: Not revealed
Fuel supply: One downdraught Solex carburettor, plus AiResearch turbocharger
Suspension: Independent front, independent rear
Weight: 4,926 lb
Top speed: 135 mph

1984 Morgan Plus 8 (with fuel injection)

Morgan styling rarely changes, and then only slightly. Unless one is a true Morgan fanatic, it would be difficult to look at almost any Plus 8 and know what decade, let along what year it was built in. Thirty years after the launch of the original Plus 8 in 1968, it still looked almost the same. Not only that, but all Plus 8s looked much like the Plus 4s of the 1950s and 1960s that they had replaced.

Yet Morgan have always had a firm grip on their market, and seem to know exactly what their customers want. Televised advice from management guru, John Harvey-Jones, that they should boost production and raise prices was ignored, and no-one complained. Production may have crawled up from 10 cars a week to about 11 cars a week, but there is still no rush at the factory at Malvern Link, a stuffed owl keeps birds out of the paint shop, and waiting lists are still measured in years.

Like the earlier Plus 4s and 4/4s, the Plus 8 was an evolutionary step on what Morgan had been doing so well for some time. Although the style, almost pre-war in concept and detail, was little changed, this time it covered a wider and longer chassis frame, and was the first

Morgan to be powered by Rover's light-alloy V8 engine.

Open two-seaters with detachable side screens, all Plus 8s used the same type of rather flexible frame, with sliding pillar independent front suspension, and rock-hard rear leaf springs. The first cars, crude in many ways because of their old-style Moss gearboxes, had 155 bhp and a 120 mph top speed, but as the years passed they were widened, became available with optional light-alloy bodies, became more refined and better equipped, and (by Morgan standards) were more sophisticated.

Later cars got five-speed Rover transmissions and wider-rim alloy wheels, the cockpit was somehow softened and equipped better, but the real advance came in 1984 when a fuel-injected 190 bhp version of the Rover engine was fitted for the first time. This, and the standardisation of rack-and-pinion steering, made the Plus 8 an even more appealing car, though the barn-door aerodynamics of the old-fashioned shape meant that no Morgan was ever likely to go faster than 130 mph.

Little, however, could be done (and there is no sign that Morgan wanted to do it, anyway) about the limited wheel movement, the hard spring and damper settings, and the creaky bodywork which tended to leak in heavy rain, though more modern Morgans had been given wooden-framed bodies steeped in preservative. The customers knew all about the problems, but they knew all about the cars' animal appeal too – and demand stayed solid. Perhaps it always will.

Below and top right: Styled much as previous models, the more powerful Plus 8 had a basic cramped interior with detachable side screens.

Morgan Plus 8

Years in production: (all types) introduced 1968
Structure: Front engine/rear-drive. Separate chassis
Engine type: V8-cylinder, over head-valve
FIRST FUEL-INJECTED VERSION:
Bore and stroke: 88.9 x 71.1 mm
Capacity: 3,528 cc
Power: 190 bhp @ 5,250 rpm
Fuel supply: Bosch-Lucas fuel injection
Suspension: Independent front, beam-axle rear
Weight: 1,900 lb
Top speed: 120 mph

1987 Lotus Esprit X180

By the end of the 20th century, the Lotus Esprit family had been on sale for nearly 25 years, which is a measure of the car's technical worth and of the original style which had been produced for Lotus by the Italian genius, Giorgetto Giugiaro. Although Lotus smoothed out the style in 1987 (to what is often known as the 'X180' shape), the car's character was not lost.

The mid-engined Esprit was designed as a replacement, but altogether larger, faster and more specialised, for the Europa, which had been Lotus's first mid-engined road car. Like the Europa, the Esprit was a two-seater with a tiny cabin mounted on a folded steel backbone chassis frame, with Lotus's own newly designed 16-valve twin-cam 2-litre engine positioned behind the cabin. The rolling chassis was wrapped in a fibreglass body full of sharp edges and planes, unmistakably from the hand of Giugiaro himself. None but a company already steeped in motor racing could ever have produced a car whose chassis promised so much, and delivered it all with such aplomb.

The first Esprits were delivered in 1976 and were cars which took time to mature, first gaining reliability and longevity, then larger engines, and finally a turbocharged version of the power unit. In 1987, with the established design well past its tenth birthday, Lotus used its in-house stylists to produce the more rounded 'X180' shape which would continue only lightly modified, to the end of the century.

In turbocharged SE form, the revised Esprit was good for around 160 mph, but there still seemed to be a demand for more performance, so in 1996 the long-rumoured Lotus 3.5-litre V8 engine, with 349 bhp, was finally introduced, making it a 175 mph car. Along the way, a whole variety of Esprit Turbos were built, some in very limited quantities, the most powerful of all being the 302 bhp variety, which traded refinement for sheer performance.

Each and every Esprit was a sports coupé with the accent on sports, majoring on function rather than convenience, for the cabin was always a snug fit for only two people, luggage space was small, and noise levels were always above average. Except that it needed a brave and expert driver to get the very best out of the chassis, no-one ever complained about the Esprit's handling, just as no-one ever seemed to find fault with the car's style and character. By the end of the 1990s, the Esprit was selling only slowly, but there were still those drivers who would not swap its agility, small size, and sheer appeal for any other.

Below: With the established Esprit design well-past its tenth birthday, Lotus produced the more rounded X180 shape which continued to the end of the century.

Lotus Esprit (X180 style)

Years in production: (All types) Introduced 1987
Structure: Mid-engine/rear-drive. Separate chassis
Engine type: 4-cylinder, twin-overhead-camshaft
Bore and stroke: 95.28 x 76.2 mm
Capacity: 2,174 cc
Power: 172 bhp @ 6,500 rpm/ 215 bhp @ 6,500 rpm
Fuel supply: Two horizontal twin-choke Dellorto carburettors/turbocharging
Suspension: Independent front, independent rear
Weight: 2,590 lb/2,800 lb
Top speed: 135 mph/150 mph

1988 Jaguar XJ-S Convertible

The original Jaguar XJ-S, which was unveiled in 1975, was the last car whose styling had been influenced by Jaguar founder Sir William Lyons before his retirement. Before it was launched, however, that style was modified to comply with US legislation. The result was that this bulky four-seater was a car which did not appeal to the same clientele as the XK, and E-type owners.

The XJ-S took its inspiration from the peerless XJ6/XJ12 saloon, for it was built around a shortened version of that car's pressed steel platform. Apart from saving a fortune in time, cost, and tooling investment, one obvious benefit was that the XJ-S also shared the same independent suspension, and the same outstanding qualities of ride and handling. No other car in the world had felt – and been – as refined as the XJ6, and the XJ-S could match it in all respects.

Like the XJ12 saloons, original XJ-Ss were all fixed-head coupés fitted with 5.3-litre V12 engines, and all but a handful had automatic transmission. Wide and squat, they were fitted with controversial 'flying buttresses' which linked the roof panel to the rear corners of the shell. Although four seats were fitted, customers rarely used them as more than spacious two-seaters with mountains of stowage space.

Very high performance and excellent ride and handling qualities had to be measured against the styling, and often ferocious thirst for fuel, but this was still a package which appealed, especially to North American buyers. Once the early quality problems had been eradicated, sales rose steadily, and the addition of 3.6-litre straight-six engines, and a clever cabriolet body style, made this a more versatile prospect.

Originally, though, there was no full convertible type. A private enterprise conversion from the USA finally persuaded Jaguar to engineer its own type which finally appeared in 1988 in V12 form. After a rear-end restyle in 1991 made the buttresses less blatant, it became even more popular in the USA, becoming the best-selling XJ-S variant. Once a more efficient 4.0-litre six-cylinder version went on sale in the early 1990s, it became another Jaguar success.

By 1996, when the XK8 finally took over from the long-running XJ-S, a total of 115,413 cars of all types had been made, of which more than 30,000 of these were XJ-S convertibles. Solid, well-engineered and reliable, they were classics from the start, and should remain so well into the 21st century.

Jaguar XJ-S Convertible
Years in production: (Convertible) 1988–96
Structure: Front engine/rear-drive. Monocoque body/chassis
Engine type: V12-cylinder, single-overhead-camshaft
Bore and stroke: 90 x 70 mm
Capacity: 5,343 cc
ORIGINAL TYPE:
Power: 291 bhp @ 5,500 rpm
Fuel supply: Bosch-Lucas fuel injection
Suspension: Independent front, independent rear
Weight: 4,055 lb
Top speed: 151 mph
Note: A 4-litre 6-cylinder version was also available from 1991.

Below: Most models were four seater, fixed-head coupés with very high performance and excellent handling qualities.

1989 Jaguar XJ220

As the prosperous 1980s unfolded, a growing number of rich car enthusiasts demanded more and more motoring excitement, so a select number of supercars were designed to satisfy them. With the exception of the McLaren F1, the mid/rear-engined Jaguar XJ220 was the fastest and most practical of all.

By any standards this was a car of huge excesses: very powerful, very fast, very beautiful, and very expensive. It was high geared and somehow bulky, so even a millionaire would not choose it for everyday use, especially as it was strictly a two-seater and, frankly, hard work to drive.

But with such exceptional good looks, no-one seemed to care. The original prototype of 1988 was only meant to be a one-off, and was even bigger than the production car which followed, using Jaguar's famous V12 engine, and four-wheel-drive. Although it had not even turned a wheel when exhibited, it carried the XJ220 title as an indication of its proposed top speed.

Jaguar XJ220

Years in production: 1992–94
Structure: Mid-engine/rear-drive. Monocoque body/chassis
Engine type: V6-cylinder, twin-overhead-camshaft
Bore and stroke: 94 x 84 mm
Capacity: 3,498 cc
Power: 542 bhp @ 7,200 rpm
Fuel supply: Zytec fuel injection, plus twin Garrett turbochargers
Suspension: Independent front, independent rear
Weight: 3,210 lb
Top speed: 213 mph

Reaction was so positive that Jaguar handed over the project to Tom Walkinshaw's Jaguar Sport organisation (with whom it was in partnership), to turn it into a reality. The 'Walkinshaw' XJ220 was shown a year later, this time significantly smaller than before, with a twin-turbo V6 engine of the type being used in current Jaguar racing sports cars, and only with rear drive.

Not that this deterred the customers, for although Jaguar said they would only build 350 cars at a newly-developed factory near Banbury, more than 1,200 customers wanted to buy one, and priority of orders had to be applied.

Built around a relatively conventional light-alloy hull, the XJ220 was really a civilised version of a race car, though with equipment which included air-conditioning and a fully-trimmed cockpit. Surprisingly, ABS anti-lock braking could not be developed in time for sales to begin in 1992.

Even though the XJ220 was tested at 213 mph, and everyone seemed to love its styling and general behaviour, Jaguar could do nothing about the general collapse in economic confidence in the early 1990s. In 1989 every customer had been obliged to sign a legal agreement when ordering the car, and to make hefty payments towards the £403,000 price, but many of them tried to wriggle out of the contract while the cars were being built.

The result was that only 271 cars were produced in three years, many of which languished un-delivered at Jaguar until the late 1990s. Amazingly, this supremely fast and beautiful Jaguar supercar now goes down in history as a commercial failure, tainted by the economic conditions of the day, rather than its own shortcomings. The question is who can possibly afford to run such a car in the future?

Below: Of all the supercars developed at the time, the XJ220 was the fastest and most practical of all. Air-conditioning was standard in the fully trimmed cockpit. The cars were extremely expensive at £403,000.

1991 TVR Griffith

Throughout its life, the TVR sports car has always lined up behind the same marketing formula – all models were two-seater sports cars, all had sturdy multi-tube chassis frames, all had fibreglass bodywork, and all had outrageously extrovert characters. Each and every car has been made in dilapidated premises in Blackpool.

The second-generation Griffith (which was no relation to an earlier TVR built in the 1960s) was faithful to every facet of the original TVR character, with one additional feature: it was outstandingly beautiful. Previous TVRs had been handsome, rugged in some cases, but none had ever achieved such sinuous styling.

This was a car which had been shaped lovingly by hand in a small workshop in Blackpool (no over-hyped consultant was ever involved, for this was the work of chairman Peter Wheeler, and his chief designer John Ravenscroft), where mundane things like bumpers were omitted from the equation, and where every straight line had been banished. Cockpit equipment was lavish, though in typical (and traditional) TVR style, the standard of fixtures and fittings were sometimes rather casually achieved.

As ever with TVR, the Griffith

TVR Griffith

Years in production: (all types) Introduced 1991
Structure: Front engine/rear-drive. Separate chassis
Engine type: V8-cylinder, over head-valve
ORIGINAL VERSION:
Bore and stroke: 94 x 77 mm
Capacity: 4,280 cc
Power: 280 bhp @ 5,500 rpm
Fuel supply: Bosch-Lucas fuel injection
Suspension: Independent front, independent rear
Weight: 2,304 lb
Top speed: 161 mph

which went on sale in 1992 was very different from the prototype of 1990, for it used a modified version of the racing Tuscan's frame. Power came from a much-modified light-alloy Rover V8, backed by the same company's sturdy five-speed transmission – and the car's specification could be boosted by larger and more powerful versions. Like all other TVRs, the Griffith had independent suspension, there was unassisted rack-and-pinion steering, four-wheel disc brakes, and large dollops of that indefinable piece of specification – character.

Early Griffiths had 280 bhp and 4.3-litres, but it wasn't long before TVR also offered a slightly milder version (with 240 bhp/4.0-litres), then from 1993 a brawny 325 bhp/5.0-litre derivative was added. Even the 4.0-litre car could top 150 mph, and the top speed of a full 5.0-litre type was best investigated on wide open spaces!

Performance was tyre-stripping, for these were cars which could rush up to 100 mph in little more than 11 seconds, the performance being accompanied by squeals from the overworked rear tyres, and aggressive bellows from the exhaust system. It was no wonder that more than 600 cars were made in the car's first full year (which made this one of the fastest-selling TVRs so far), and it was only the advent of new and even more extrovert TVRs which thrust the Griffiths back into the mainstream.

Below: The TVR Griffith had no bumpers front or back and the interior trimmings were lavish. Shaped lovingly by hand, the car bodywork was made from glassfibre and was full of character.

1992 Ford Escort RS Cosworth

When Ford-UK needed a new rally car for World Championship use in the 1990s, it combined the best of Sierra engineering, the best of Cosworth's engine-tuning expertise, and a brave approach to aerodynamics, to produce the Escort RS Cosworth. Although this car looked something like the mainstream front-drive Escort of day, it had a four-wheel-drive chassis, and hid much Sierra RS Cosworth heritage under its bewinged skin.

Starting on the basis of a shortened Sierra Cosworth 4x4 platform, and adapting a three-door Escort body superstructure to that, Ford spent time in its wind tunnels, eventually endowing the new car with a large and entirely functional rear spoiler. This, along with other add-ons, louvres and detail changes, produced a car which not only looked aggressively purposeful, but which developed positive downforce at high speeds. As speeds rose, the car was actually pressed further down onto its suspension, loading up the tyres and increasing potential grip.

With 227 bhp available from its 2-litre turbocharged engine in standard form, the Escort RS Cosworth was already a comfortable, reliable, exhilarating and extremely capable road car, but with 300 bhp or more, and a whole host of extra equipment in place, it became a phenomenal rally car. Road cars, equipped with fat and soft-compound Pirelli P Zero tyres, handled like no previous Ford had ever done, and because they were so small and agile, they soon attracted a cult following. The looks, perhaps, were an acquired taste, but no-one ever argued about the abilities of the package.

Ford Escort RS Cosworth

Years in production: 1992–96
Structure: Front engine/four-wheel-drive. Monocoque body/chassis
Engine type: 4-cylinder, twin-over head-camshaft
Bore and stroke: 90.82 x 76.95 mm
Capacity: 1,993 cc
Power: 227 bhp @ 6,250 rpm
Fuel supply: Weber-Marelli fuel injection, with Garrett turbocharger
Suspension: Independent front, independent rear
Weight: 2,882 lb
Top speed: 137 mph

Right: Although it resembled the mainstream Escorts of the day, the Escort RS Cosworth had four-wheel-drive and an aerodynamic shape.

Road cars went on sale in 1992, cars started winning World Championship rallies in 1993, and by 1995 this had become one of the most successful Ford competition cars of all time. Victory in the Monte Carlo Rally (in 1994 and 1996) established the car's reputation for good, and in a final evolution, as the Escort WRC rally car, it was good enough for Carlos Sainz to win several world-class events.

The problem, as so often with these cars, is that the Escort RS Cosworth was too costly (£23,500 at first) to appeal to the mass market, too complex for Ford's dealer chain to understand, and far too special for the companies who had to insure it, so Ford never sold more than about 3,000 cars in a year. The final version, shorn of its big spoiler and with a small turbocharger, was a better road car, but not ideal for use in motorsport.

Commercial success, however, was never the most important factor in this charismatic car's career. By the time the last one was built in 1996, Ford enthusiasts had already christened it a classic, had found ways of extracting up to 400 bhp from its engine, and were defying Ford to produce even better cars in the future.

Right: One of Ford's most successful Rally cars of all time, the Escort RS Cosworth.

1993 McLaren F1

At the end of the 1980s, the fashion for making and marketing supercars with colossal performance was short-lived. At a time when rich men had money to splash around, supercars were very popular, but as recession followed, the market for expensive fast cars collapsed. All the cars in this class, such as the Bugatti EB110 and the Jaguar XJ220, could easily beat 200 mph, but few owners ever found a place to exercise that top speed. The McLaren F1 was probably the best of this exclusive breed – not only did it have a top speed of 230 mph and more, but it was stylish rather than brutally sexy, beautifully engineered and built with a unique layout.

McLaren, already famous for its Grand Prix cars, invited ex-Brabham F1 designer Gordon Murray to join them at Woking, where he concentrated on the new road-car product, which they decided, confusingly, to call 'F1'. Predictably enough, he laid out a mid-engined coupé, but there were important differences. Not only did McLaren persuade BMW to develop a unique alloy 627 bhp/6.1-litre V12 engine to power the car, but Murray laid out the interior as a three-seater, where the driver sat in the middle, ahead of his two passengers.

To keep the weight down, every possible high-tech. aerospace standard material was used: this was the world's first carbon-fibre chassised road car, and similar materials cropped up in detail all round the car – and the performance was stupendous. No British source, not even McLaren, could test the 230 mph-plus top speed in the UK, so a trip to the enormous circular test track at Nardo in southern Italy was made to prove the point. As expected, though, the acceleration figures were outstanding (and, as the climate for motoring has changed, may never be surpassed). The F1 could sprint from rest to 100 mph in 6.3 seconds, and to 200 mph in a mere 28 seconds. All this was accompanied by average fuel consumption of better than 15 mpg, the driver achieving it all in air-conditioned comfort.

Although the F1 was not meant to be a car for everyday use (significantly, it lacked features such as ABS braking, and power-assisted steering), it was small enough (only 71.6 in/1,820 mm wide) and light enough at 2,510 lb/1,138 kg, to be used in heavy traffic, or in normal conditions, but this was to waste the potential of a magnificent machine.

Even McLaren would now admit that it arrived on the market too late, for at the huge price of £540,000, it was never likely to sell in significant numbers. Although thousands of enthusiasts were impressed by it, very few (all multi-millionaires) bought an F1. After less than four years, in which only 100 cars (including a large proportion of special racing versions) were built, McLaren brought this loss-making project to a close. For sheer performance, such a car, it is thought, will never be beaten.

Right: The world's first carbon-fibre chassis road car. A three-seater, the driver sat in the middle ahead of his two passengers. Capable of 100 mph in 6.3 seconds from rest.

McLaren F1

Years in production: 1993–98
Structure: Mid-engine/rear-drive. Monocoque body/chassis
Engine type: V12-cylinder, twin-overhead-camshaft
Bore and stroke: 86 x 87 mm
Capacity: 6,064 cc
Power: 627 bhp @ 7,400 rpm
Fuel supply: Bosch fuel injection
Suspension: Independent front, independent rear
Weight: 2,509 lb
Top speed: 230 mph +

1995 MG MGF

By the 1970s, British Leyland was in such a financial mess that several factories had to be closed down, one of them being the MG plant at Abingdon. This meant the death of the long-running MGB – and the end of MG sports car production for more than a decade. After several changes of control in the 1980s, British Leyland became Rover, who were determined to revive MG sports cars. The retro-engineered MG RV8 of 1992 was the first new model, but it was the all-new mid-engined MGF of 1995 which caused such a stir.

By any previous MG standards, the layout of the new MGF was sensational enough, but the commercial deal which made the project viable was equally bold. Rover planned to make only 15,000 cars a year and needed an investment partner. They found it in the Mayflower business of Coventry, which not only produced all the body shell tooling and built all the bodies, but financed that operation too.

Sleek, rounded, compact and arranged purely as a two-seater, the MGF had a new unit-construction body shell, with all-independent suspension, but (in the very best historic MG traditions) almost all the engine, transmission and chassis components were lifted, only slightly modified, from mass production family cars in the parent company. The twin-cam four-cylinder engine was a highly-tuned version of the 16-valve K-series units already found in Rover 100, 200 and 400 models, and was linked to a neat, five-speed transmission, the entire assembly being placed closely behind the passenger cabin. There were two engine tunes, the most powerful having technically advanced VVC, or Variable (Timing) Valve Control. Hydragas suspension, interconnected from front to rear, as used in the Rover 100

(the former Metro) was modified to include separate telescopic dampers and anti-roll bars at each end of the car, which ensured sports car handling allied to a soft and supple ride. Rack-and-pinion steering was as expected, though not the speed-sensitive electric power assistance which was also available.

By any standards this was a fast and well equipped little car, which kept its high performance (131 mph on the VVC-engined cars) in check with four-wheel discs, and ABS braking on the VVC version. Fuel injection, electric windows, a catalytic converter and part leather trimming in the cockpit made it an appealing little car which sold well – and continued to sell – from the moment it went on sale.

British customers originally had to pay £15,995 for the 'base' car, £17,995 for the VVC-engined machine, but there were waiting lists at first. For the first time, though, this was an MG sports car which was not to be sold in the USA. Five years after its launch, the MGF had gained a detachable hard-top option, but few other changes, and it looked exactly the same as in 1995. The co-financing deal had already paid off handsomely, and for the 2000s its future looks secure.

MG MGF

Years in production: Introduced 1995
Structure: Mid-engine/rear-drive. Monocoque body/chassis
Engine type: 4-cylinder, twin-over-head-camshaft
Bore and stroke: 80 x 89.3 mm
Capacity: 1,795 cc
Power: 118/143 bhp @ 5,500/7,000 rpm
Fuel supply: Lucas fuel injection
Suspension: Independent front, independent rear
Weight: 2,366 lb
Top speed: 123/131 mph

Below: Sleek, rounded and compact, the new lay-out of the MG MGF caused a stir at its launch.

The mid-engined MG MGF traces its ancestry all the way back to the MG 14/28 of 1926, a living embodiment of the British Classic Car.